Intermi ... *16/8*

The Complete Guide To Fasting And Weight Loss

Dorota Perkins

2021

Intermittent Fasting 16/8

The Complete Guide To
Fasting And Weight Loss

Polish Edition: February 2020
English Edition: November 2021

Author
Dorota Perkins

Copy Editor
Caitlin Owen

Content Editor
Klaudia Koscielecka

Translated from Polish
Mateusz Wawrzynowicz

ISBN *(paperback) 978-1-7398472-0-3*
ISBN *(eBook) 978-1-7398472-1-0*

TABLE OF CONTENTS

TABLE OF CONTENTS

Introduction

In 2016, Japanese scientist Yoshinori Ohsumi was awarded the Nobel Prize for his discovery of short-term fasting. His fame spread quickly, and suddenly the world realised that this was something worth trying. Intermittent Fasting (or 'IF'), a simple solution for reducing food consumption hours, has become one of the most popular nutrition methods worldwide and is constantly gaining popularity.

In both 2018 and 2019, a report from the International Food Information Council Foundation concluded that Intermittent Fasting was the world's most popular nutrition method.

IF is fascinating for many reasons: it is a method that guarantees rapid weight loss and has a remarkable effect on both the regulation of our hormonal balance and detoxification of our body. It is a dietary method that costs nothing, so people who use it also find themselves effortlessly saving a lot of money.

In the world of science, IF is currently at the centre of attention. Great scientists, such as Professor Valter Longo, Professor Yoshinori Ohsumi, Jason Fung, MD, and many, many others, are constantly researching and improving the assumptions of IF.

When writing this book, I wanted to present how to put this method into practice step by step, and explain the scientific basis of weight loss in the light of IF in a clear and simple manner. Throughout the book, I elaborate on critical hormonal processes in the body. Understanding these processes will enable you to succeed in losing weight.

You will also learn about how stress affects your weight, how to break down your goals so that you can achieve them more easily, what mindfulness training is, and how to do it. This book is a holistic compendium of knowledge and motivation, that will allow you to find all the answers to your questions in a single place.

A few years ago, I was overcome by a dramatic need for some change in my life. I knew that I was getting older and that it was time to take another look at myself, my life, and my diet. What did I do? I started googling. I typed in "lifestyle", "change", "new ways of thinking", "philosophy", and "for whom the bell tolls" in the search engine (just joking with that last one!). I remember that something along the lines of "Intermittent Fasting Lifestyle" popped up in the search results on my laptop's monitor. The results intrigued me. I can still remember the feeling of relief as I started reading and taking in information.

Here's what I found out:
1: You don't have to eat breakfast!
2: You don't need to eat five meals a day!

I sat in my chair for a few minutes. Suddenly it arose that my dislike of having breakfast straight after waking up was scientifically justified! It also became apparent that I did not have to spend the rest of my free time preparing food. After all, I would rather spend these moments with my family instead of preparing meals for some miracle diet! From that day on, my life changed forever.

In December 2017, I founded a support group called "Intermittent Fasting 16: 8 - Poland - Intermittent Fasting - 8-hour diet". In less than two years, the group has become the largest Facebook community in Poland devoted to this subject matter. It is a community of several thousand amiable, mutually supportive people, who will tell you what an amazing influence IF had on their lives.

I personally witnessed some remarkable metamorphoses, not only in appearance but also in lifestyle, health, and way of thinking. These changes were not only temporary but lasted a lifetime.

You will learn some great stories from the people in this community who agreed to share their success in this book, to help you find a better way of life and inspire you.

Thank you all!

Thanks

This book would not have been written if it had not been for the wonderful community of several thousand people belonging to the "Intermittent Fasting 16: 8 - Poland - Intermittent Fasting - 8-hour diet" group. The group has always motivated me to broaden my horizons and answer essential questions concerning Intermittent Fasting. I would also like to thank you for supporting me during the process of writing this book. Thank you all!

Thank you to my moderators - Renata, Arek, and Aga - for the knowledge that you share with the group.

Wanting to ensure that this book contains 100% facts and that no mistakes have crept in, I asked Klaudia Kościelecka and Caitlin Owen to read it and make any necessary corrections - thank you both for the time you took to correct the book.

I want to thank my friend Ania Wojtczak for helping me prepare the material about protein and fat breakfasts and for invaluable support during my many months of work on the book.

I would not have written this book if it had not been for the support of my family: my mother, Franciszka, who has always believed in me, and my niece, Karolina, who watched over the correctness of the references.

And finally, the two most important people in my life - my husband Andy and daughter Emilia - thank you for your love and understanding.

Important!

This book was written for healthy adults.
The author of this book is not a medical doctor
but a populariser of knowledge.

Whenever you make any changes to your diet or
nutritional habits, it is always a good idea to
consult your GP first.

Enjoy your reading!

Dorota Perkins

IF gives me freedom
IF gives me a choice
IF gives me tranquillity of mind
IF gives me energy
IF gives me rest
IF gives me knowledge
IF gives me mental clarity
IF gives me LIFESTYLE

Dorota Perkins

What is Intermittent Fasting?

Intermittent Fasting (or IF) is one of the most popular health trends in the world. It consists of alternating between fasting and eating periods. There are many different varieties of IF, such as 16: 8, 5: 2, Eat Stop Eat, OMAD, 24-72h fasting, and many more.

It should be mentioned here that IF is not a diet but a way of nutrition. IF does not define what to eat, but how to eat and how to fast. Therefore, you can combine IF with a diet of your choice - ketogenic, carnivore, or any other diet that suits you.

IF protects against many diseases. This is because it regulates numerous bodily processes, including our hormonal balance. Fasting also regulates insulin sensitivity. Eating too many carbohydrates - especially simple sugars - can lead to insulin resistance, which in turn contributes to the development of chronic diseases, including type II diabetes.

If your goal is to get rid of tummy fat, Intermittent Fasting is also a great solution.

What does the scientific world say about Intermittent Fasting?

In 2016, a Japanese scientist was awarded the Nobel Prize for his discoveries about autophagy, which is directly related to the processes taking place during IF. You will find out more about this throughout this book.

In 2018, the Food Information Council Foundation presented a report that showed that IF is the most popular nutritional method globally.

Scientific research has also shown that IF is an excellent weight-loss tool. In 2015, scientists proved that fasting every other day for 3-12 weeks can lead to significant weight loss - up to 5.5 kg of body fat alone.

Another scientific study was conducted on 71 volunteers who fasted for 5 days a week with only 750-1100 calories a day. The participants repeated the routine every three months for three cycles, which led to an average loss of about 3 kg of body fat without sacrificing any muscle mass. The study found that overall inflammation in the body had also decreased.

Published in the 'World Journal of Diabetics', another scientific report showed that IF among people with type II diabetes significantly improved important indicators such as body weight and blood glucose levels.

Finally, one investigation proved that IF was just as effective in lowering the body fat surrounding internal organs as decreasing calory intake is. If you suffer from a prediabetic state or have problems with insulin sensitivity, IF was proved to help regulate these problems.

Live forever!

Studies on rats have shown that IF extended their lives. One study indicated that by reducing body fat through the use of IF increased their lifespan. Another study on mice found that fatter mice lived longer because of the use of IF, and slimmer ones that were not fed in accordance with the rules of IF lived shorter lives. Of course, there have been no studies on humans concerning the relationship between IF and life expectancy yet, but animal studies are very promising.

The most popular types of Intermittent Fasting

- ### *The 16/8 method and its variants:*

The most common form of IF is 16: 8. These numbers indicate that we fast for 16 hours and eat within an 8-hour window. Therefore, eating and fasting over a 24-hour period.

It's important to remember that the fasting hours are indicated first, followed by the number that determines our eating window. I have often seen IF beginners use these numbers in reverse order, which can lead to unnecessary confusion!

Other popular forms/variations of 16: 8 are: 14: 10, 18: 6, 20: 4, 22: 2, or 23: 1, which is more commonly known as OMAD (or 'one meal a day'). OMAD follows the rule that everything we want to eat is consumed within one hour.

As you may have noticed, fasting takes place within 24 hours each time, i.e., one day. The varieties of IF mentioned above are determined by the degree of training in IF, or personal preferences.

You can use 16: 8 continually, throughout all stages of your life. A lot of people have followed this style of eating for many years, some even saying that they have used 16: 8 unknowingly throughout their lives.

- ### *The 5:2 method:*

This method is very well-known and has become famous thanks to TV shows and books by Michael Moseley, MD. 5: 2 is all about eating around 800 calories a day during two selected days of the week. In the previous 5: 2 version, 500 calories were recommended - however, the new version of this method permits 800 calories. On the other days of the week, we follow our normal (but rational!) diet.

- ### *The Eat Stop Eat method:*

  The Eat Stop Eat method was invented by Brad Pilon, who, after finishing his studies, researched short fasting periods. In his approach to IF, Brad Pilon recommends two 24-hour fasts in one week. At the same time, he advises a reasonably rational diet during the other five days. You can decide for yourself when you want to fast and when you would rather eat. There is also no limit to the number of meals.

Intermittent Fasting is not for everyone

Intermittent fasting is not for:

- children

- people who are underweight

- people with an eating disorder or a history of eating disorders

- pregnant women

- many nursing women

- many people with a medical diagnosis

- many people taking medication.

Before starting IF, you should ask your GP if it is safe to embark on this eating journey.

Fasting in ancient medicine and religions of the world.

Ancient medicine

It could seem as though fasting is an invention of the 21st century - but it isn't. Many ancient physicians recommended fasting both to prevent disease and accelerate recovery.

One of the most prolific doctors of ancient times, Hippocrates, was also a great supporter of fasting. He is known to us primarily as the father of medicine and the author of the *primum non nocere* principle - that is: "first, do no harm".

Hippocrates was born around 460 BC and died roughly around 377 BC, which means that he lived for approximately 83 years.[42] Quite a long time in ancient times! Hippocrates was a great supporter of fasting and used its therapeutic properties in his medical practice. He believed that fasting enables the body to heal. In his own words: "Everyone has a doctor in him or her; we just have to help it in its work. The natural healing force within each one of us is the greatest force in getting well. (...) But to eat when you are sick, is to feed your sickness."[59]

Another well-known figure, but from the AD era, was Paracelsus - a city physician from Basel born in 1493. He was a doctor and naturalist and was named the father of modern medicine.[43] His fame mostly stemmed from his research on producing medicine for syphilis. Although fasting was not the cure for syphilis, as you can imagine, its use was something that he appreciated in his practice. In his works, which were wrote over 500 years ago, he indicated that fasting is the best medicine. He stated:

"Fasting is the greatest remedy – the physician within."[59]

While searching for other sayings and quotes uttered by famous doctors or philosophers regarding fasting, I found hundreds of them. Here are a few of my favourites:

"Instead of using medicine, better fast today." - Plutarch

"The best of all medicines are resting and fasting." - Benjamin Franklin

"I fast for greater physical and mental efficiency." - Plato [59]

The Catholic Church

Fasting has always been an integral part of many religions, including Christianity. Fasting is also observed in the Catholic Church.

The days of fasting are usually named Ash Wednesday and Good Friday. During fasting, you should not eat meat or meat products, and you should also limit your meals. In some places, fasting entails only consuming one full meal during the day.

To my great surprise, while researching information regarding fasting in the Catholic Church, I found that there are at least four types of fasting: qualitative, quantitative, strict, and Eucharistic – and what's more, each of them have specific rules assigned. I was also taken aback to find that fasting is governed by a 'code of law' - in this case, the 1917 Code of Canon Law. The code determines the age of individuals who are required to fast. Interestingly, it applies to everyone from the age of 18 until the age of 60. You can read a quote from the Code of Canon Law below[44]:

"The law of abstinence binds those who have completed their fourteenth year. The law of fasting binds those who have attained their majority, until the beginning of their sixtieth year. Pastors of souls and parents are to ensure that even those who by reason of their age are not bound by the law of fasting and abstinence, are taught the true meaning of penance." (can. 1252)[45]

The Bible

There are many quotes in the Bible about fasting. To understand more about fasting in relation to the Bible, you can read the texts found at www.bibliamowi.pl. You will find a lot of relevant information about fasting there, including the mention that "(...) Fasting in the Bible has many roles and is not limited to abstaining from eating. It is a special time of getting closer to God, a time of studying the Holy Scriptures, prayers, requests, and answers..."[46]

In the Holy Scriptures, there are references to intercessory fasting, ancillary fasting, strengthening fasting, penance fasting, spiritual fasting, and partial fasting. Jesus' fasting is probably the most well-known variation. The Bible reads:

"Then Jesus was led by the Spirit into the wilderness to be tempted by the devil. After fasting forty days and forty nights, he was hungry. The tempter came to him and said: If you are the Son of God, tell these stones to become bread." Mt 4,1-3 (BT)

The theme of fasting is known in all religions around the world, except for one, Zoroastrianism, which forbids it.

The Orthodox Church

Orthodox Christians believe that fasting helps to cleanse themselves of their sins and take care of the salvation of their souls. During the 40 days of Lent, Orthodox Christians do not eat meat, fish, eggs, or dairy products.[48]
The period of Lent in the Orthodox Church is movable. The sacrament of marriage is not administered in the Orthodox Church during this time. Also, no food should be eaten on the first Monday and Tuesday of Orthodox Lent, hence the naming of these days as 'Clean Monday' and 'Clean Tuesday'. In addition, fasting applies before Christmas, the Feast of Saints Peter and Paul, and the Feast of the Dormition of the Mother of God. There are also one-day fasting periods[49].

Judaism

Judaism mentions six days of fasting. Fasting periods in this religion can be divided into two areas: those that apply to everyone, and those that are observed by individual people. Yom Kippur and Tisha B'Av last 24 hours, from sunset to the next. However, before Purim and Pesach, followers fast from sunrise to sunset. Individual fasting periods are adhered to mainly within the setting of the family circle. For example, children observe them on the anniversary of their parents' death, and young couples during their wedding.[60]

Islam

"O you who believe, the fasts have been enjoined upon you as they were enjoined upon those before you, so that you may be God-fearing." (Quran 2: 183)

Fasting is one of the five pillars of Islam. Ramadan is the main fast for Muslims, that lasts for a month each year and is mandatory. Ramadan is about abstaining from food and liquids from sunrise to sunset. The purpose of fasting is to cleanse the body in order to receive the spirit of godliness and justice. It is a time of reckoning and reflection.

"(...) Fasting in the month of Ramadan - the ninth month of the Muslim calendar - lasts 29 or 30 days. Ramadan is a particular time for all Muslims - it is a month of unique contact with God, self-discipline, and reflection. People who fast, experiencing thirst and hunger, show solidarity with hungry individuals all over the world. This month should be additionally filled with prayer and good deeds (...)".[47]

Buddhism

Fasting in Buddhism is seen primarily as a method of self-control, but also a path to liberation. Monks and nuns often eat only one meal a day, which is in the morning. The Buddha advised the monks not to eat food in the afternoon. While experiencing extreme asceticism, he recognised the 'Middle Way', which is expected to prevent monks from enjoying the pleasures of life excessively. The Buddha was also opposed to extreme mortification. The ideal solution is therefore moderation, or the 'Middle Way'.

Quite an intriguing form of fasting in Buddhism shows monks asking for food, while they carry an empty bowl. If a monk is not given anything to eat, he will then not be able to eat at all. Buddhist practitioners not only fast by restricting their food, but they also do it through sacrifice. They try to sacrifice something of their own for the world, and for other people.[49]

Is it true that Intermittent Fasting received the Nobel Prize? And what is autophagy?

The basic assumption behind the autophagy process is that when a stressor is revealed, the body starts self-devouring, which is where the word autography is derived from. (From the Greek "autos" - self and "phagein" - to devour).

Scientists have stated that autophagy is essential in defending our bodies against chronic, metabolic, and neurological diseases. If the autophagy process is disturbed or inoperable, toxins accumulate, and we get ill.

Our understanding of the autophagy process dates to 1963, and is attributed to a Belgian biochemist, Christian de Duve. While examining the liver tissue, de Duve noticed special bubbles in the cells that deal with disposal or recycling, which were named lysosomes. Lysosomes - with the help of appropriate enzymes - digest dead and damaged tissue, bacteria, proteins, viruses, and other waste.

At first, de Duve was concerned about this phenomenon and thought that something was wrong with the cell, because he found it disturbing that it contained something self-destructive. He quickly realized however, lysosomes break down old and unnecessary cells into amino acids, which in turn are used to build new cell structures.

Christian de Duve was awarded the Nobel Prize for his discoveries in 1974[1]. However, the understanding of autophagy developed significantly in 2016. Yoshinori Ohsumi, a Japanese biologist, received the Nobel Prize for his research into the mechanisms governing autophagy. By conducting research on yeast, he discovered that specific stressors, including fasting, trigger autophagy[2].

His later research showed that a similar phenomenon occurs in animals and humans when they lack nutrients. Yoshinori concluded that the energy generated by self-devouring is used to build new functional cells[3].

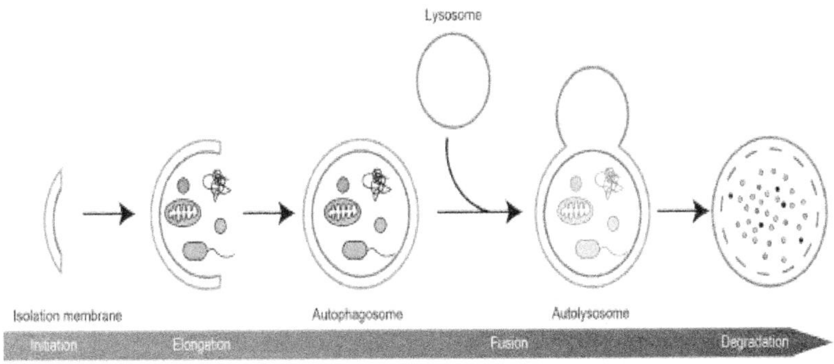

Photo 1. *This is what autophagy looks like at the cellular level.*

As shown in the diagram above[2], an autophagosome that contains damaged materials will bind to a phagosome. The phagosome has been activated due to stress, such as starvation or lack of nutrients. The phagosome then leads to the degradation or recycling of the material contained in the autophagosome, while the two elements are combining. The material contains remnants of dead cells, toxins, and bacteria[4].

To explain it in a simpler way, the phenomenon presented in the diagram above can be compared to cleaning your home, car, or workplace. It is not hard to imagine what would happen if we stopped throwing out the rubbish or looking after our house. We would be drowning in a mess of debris and rotting food, and rats would most likely appear in our household.

Following our analogy, IF can be compared to dusting our house and keeping everything in order. When we do not eat for at least 13-16 hours, we maintain this order – homeostasis in our body at the cellular level.

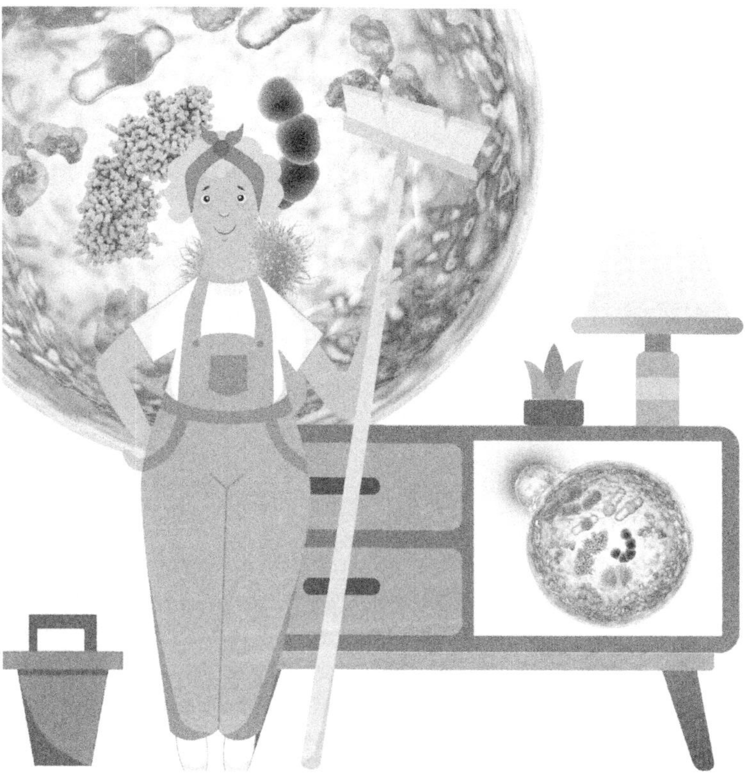

However, we know very well what cleaning is like - we all need to perform general cleaning from time to time. We should extend these 16 hours to 18, 20, or maybe even 24 hours once a week. Only then will we be sure that when the mother-in-law visits, she will not give us a hard time, and our house will shine.

What about Christmas or other special occasions? After all, we would not like to disappoint our mother-in-law, so we clean behind our wardrobes or wash the carpets. In short, we turn everything upside down and clean it once or twice a year. In terms of fasting then, we should think about a more extended fasting period - at least 24 hours, once or twice a year.

Remember, there are no predetermined rules on how often you clean your house or whether you want to extend your fast - the choice is yours. But be aware, you need to make your body accustomed to fasting at first. Once you feel you can tolerate the lack of food for 16 hours, you can think about lengthening your fasting period.

Later on in this book, we'll talk about how to introduce and extend your fast gradually. Scientific research shows that fasting from 24 to 72 hours while drinking water gives great results in terms of autophagy. As previously described, it's essential to clean our outer environment but also the internal one. The autophagy process that takes place during IF helps us get rid of deformed, malformed proteins that have a toxic effect on our internal environment[6].

Eric Berg believes that IF helps puts insulin in check, thus reducing insulin resistance. Supposing we stick to the principles of IF, we will be able to significantly reduce the degree of deposition of deformed proteins in the body. Our bodies will defend themselves against toxic metabolites.

If you have been wondering whether a low-carb diet is vital during IF, you have probably now found your answer. However, this does not mean that you have to go to extremes. Of course, many of you may need time to gradually cut down on simple carbohydrates in your diet.

On the other hand, consuming too much and having an unspent amount of protein in our diet can also cause problems with initiating autophagy. William Dunn, a professor of anatomy and cell physiology, and lecturer at the University of Florida, has been working on autophagy for thirty years. In one of his interviews, he thoroughly discusses the advantages of autophagy during IF. He explains that the body, deprived of amino acids and proteins for many hours, will consequently initiate the processes of autophagy[7].

Dunn admits that he uses autophagy as a means of having a healthier heart[5]. He explains that autophagy must be activated for all cells that do not divide, and that it can also significantly improve health in any relatively healthy person. However, autophagy can have an undesirable effect in people who already have broken down disease cells, such as certain forms of cancer[9].

We should think about how to effectively improve the chances of initiating autophagy in our bodies during IF. A famous specialist in the field of IF, Mindy Pelz, offers several effective methods. These techniques that will help us to accelerate the phenomenon of autophagy are as follows:

First of all, start by lowering your glycogen levels. As you may know, glycogen is produced from carbohydrates that are supplied to the body with food. Glycogen is stored in the liver and muscles. This is where the use of IF and a low-carb diet would be a crucial mechanism to help us achieve autophagy. We need to keep the protein levels as low as possible, due to an enzyme called mTOR kinase.

Exercising in the gym or interval training will be useful here, as it will weaken mTor kinase and improve lymphatic flow. We should also stimulate another enzyme - AMPK kinase, which - among other things - tells the body to start taking energy from stored fat. Drinking green tea, coffee, turmeric, ginger, or elderberry can help with this.

Mindy Pelz believes that after just 13 hours of fasting, our body stops storing fat and begins to use it, burning it off. At the same time, a significant increase in the concentration of growth hormone also begins[8].

Growth hormone causes the aging processes to be delayed, and makes fat burn at the same time. Pelz explains that after 16 hours, the process in which the body switches to consuming its own toxins by activating autophagy begins. Therefore, it is recommended that you fast for a minimum of 16 hours to start benefiting from this wonderful process. Pelz continues to explain that many of her patients eat only one meal a day, which gives them fantastic weight loss results. She recommends that if someone wants to utilise old fat deposits, a 36-hour fasting period while periodically drinking water will be a great solution.

In turn, Jason Fung, MD, claims that effective autophagy will occur between the 24th and 48th hour of fasting, while drinking water. He also believes that autophagy may begin much earlier than expected if you are already on a low carb diet and a low protein level. As previously mentioned, the processes start with a fasting time of around 16 hours, and the best results can be obtained by extending this period. You can also apply the principle of general cleaning.

Weight loss is the most significant motivator for people who want to start IF. However, we need to understand what is happening in our bodies. Autophagy is an important topic when trying to understand the surprising effectiveness of IF. More and more often, in various media types, we hear that IF has received a Nobel Prize. We can state that self-devouring, i.e., our body's self-repair, occurs under the influence of starvation.

Finally, with some nostalgia, I will quote the words of Nobel laureate Professor Yoshimoro Oshumi, who pointed out that we do not yet know much about autophagy. We may have only discovered 15% - 30% of the facts on this topic. I would like to believe that although this is a small percentage of knowledge, we will use it as best as possible.

Growth hormone

When we discussed autography, you may remember the growth hormone being mentioned. We know that its concentration rises sharply after 13 hours of fasting. However, to begin this chapter, let's explore what the human growth hormone is and clarify its importance during IF.

Growth hormone (GH), also known as somatropin, is produced naturally by our body in the anterior pituitary gland. Once released into the bloodstream, it remains active for only a few minutes. Despite this, it is vital in the process of growth and proper functioning of the body.

This hormone is responsible for growth in children and adolescents, so we see high levels in this period of life. Even so, GH is still present in adults whose growth period has already ended, although it has slightly different functions. It affects, among other things, building muscle mass, metabolism, and fat burning.

It is worth mentioning that there is also a synthetic form of this hormone used to treat certain conditions, including dwarfism and growth hormone deficiency. Throughout the world, synthetic GH is often used as a dopant in sport. It should be noted here that there are also differences in the level of GH secretion between women and men.

GH helps build muscle strength, which can also improve the quality of your strength exercises. If you combine strength training with IF, you will have a fantastic tool to burn fat and build muscle tissue. So, if you were wondering if it is OK to exercise during fasting, you can be assured it is both safe and effective.

One scientific study showed that the concentration of growth hormone was increased by as much as 300% after three days of fasting, and by 1250% after a one-week fast! Furthermore, another study also confirmed similar effects after 2-3 days of fasting[14].

However, it should be mentioned that fasting for a few days consecutively is much more difficult. IF in the 16: 8 system is a preferable choice since we fast every day. Such a system makes it easier to utilise fasting as a lifestyle, that will ensure higher levels of GH after just 13 hours of well-done fasting.

Research confirms that an increased concentration of GH will help you lose stored fat. Eric Berg, a specialist in weight loss, assumes that people with low levels of this hormone tend to put on weight. He also indicates that the secretion of this hormone drops dramatically in women after the age of 50. It is worth remembering that women generally have lower GH levels than men, which is why IF is a great tool for women to use.

Increased secretion of GH occurs alongside a decrease in insulin levels in the bloodstream. At this point, the amount of glycogen stored in the liver is depleted. IF will help you keep your insulin levels low and keep your growth hormone levels high. Elevated insulin levels can disrupt this process, so consider this before adding anything to water, coffee, or tea during fasting periods.

You should also keep in mind that exercise supports the secretion of GH and accelerates autophagy. Fasting has been proven to have positive effects on muscle mass and other markers. This is mainly because, due to the natural production of GH, fasting significantly accelerates fat loss while your muscle tissue is growing. Traditionally, athletes are advised to consume large amounts of protein half an hour after exercising to build muscle mass and reduce body fat. Fasting is usually advised to them during training days, whereas eating is recommended during competitions.

A couple of great examples of the positive results of IF are Łukasz Litwa and Apc Arkadiusz Paweł Cielas. They are members of my group devoted to IF. They have achieved outstanding results relatively quickly - using IF, strength exercises, and a properly balanced diet during eating periods. You will see their stories along with photos later in this book.

Some IF practitioners may have noticed stronger nails or faster-growing hair. These changes are by no means an illusion! Our hair and nails are constantly growing and need to be properly nourished, like many other tissues. It is proteins that determine the volume and thickness of the hair, and strength of the nails.

Not everyone knows that the basic building block of hair and nails is a protein named keratin. The concentration of GH has a positive effect on the level of keratin in our bodies. Hair can consist of up to 90% of the amino acids that are part of keratin. Eric Berg mentions this phenomenon in one of his recordings.

In turn, Stephanie Edmondson, PhD, working at the University of Melbourne, is involved in GH research. She has conducted an extensive review of scientific papers about the effects GH has on our skin. The results indicate that many scientific studies confirm the crucial role of GH and insulin-like growth factors (IGF) in the formation of healthy skin.

Edmondson suggests that any disruptions in secretion can lead to diseases and significant skin changes. They may include diseases such as psoriasis or neoplastic lesions at the epidermal level. Most of the studies covered in Edmondson's review suggest that insulin-like growth factors play a direct role in maintaining epidermal homeostasis.

Eric Berg lists five factors that stimulate the secretion of GH in a natural way. The very first one he mentions is IF. He then points to the importance of keeping low sugar levels in your diet. Berg also mentions the amino acid arginine, and shows its positive effect on the secretion of GH. The primary sources of arginine are meat, dairy products, and some plant-based foods. As the fourth factor, Berg talks about vitamin D3, which we can find in fatty fish, cheese, and healthy sun rays. The last factor that positively influences GH is interval exercises, for instance HIIT.

Growth hormone and lack of sleep

The significance of good sleep is often underestimated when it comes to effective weight loss. Few people know that lack of sleep directly impacts problems with gaining weight, but it does! Experts estimate that as much as 75% of growth hormone is secreted during sleep[17]. GH is released in phase 3 of sleep, i.e., more than an hour after falling asleep. This phase is also known as deep sleep.

Blood flow in the deep sleep phase is directed from the brain to muscles, to aid recovery and increase energy. The secreted GH enhances regeneration and reconstruction in our bodies. Interrupted sleep disrupts sleep phases and consequently has a negative effect on GH secretion. On the other hand, if you are awake all night, and this is normal for you, GH will not be released. This process will take place only when you manage to fall asleep after a sleepless night.

In a study, scientists conducted an experiment where they separated volunteers from daylight and other clues suggesting the time of day. The volunteers were able to plan their own bedtime, which consequently deviated from a regular 24-hour cycle of the day. They slept at different times, not knowing, of course, whether it was night or day. It turned out that GH was secreted in smaller amounts even though its levels should have been much higher.

Thus, the researchers concluded that the length of the sleep phases had an impact on the amount of GH secreted. Since as much as 75% of GH is secreted during sleep, it is vital to take care of sleep hygiene. Unfortunately, we do not have much choice if we work night shifts and must sleep during the day. However, we must try to sleep whenever we can to benefit from GH secretion as much as possible. Otherwise, our hormonal balance may be unstable, which will translate into worse results of weight loss.

IGF-1

So, what is IGF-1? Well, the abbreviation comes from the English name ‘insulin-like growth factor’. Remember when I mentioned that the pituitary gland secretes GH? When the pituitary gland produces GH, it travels to the liver, and the liver produces IGF-1. The effects of IGF-1 are very similar to those of GH. It is almost like comparing GH to a director and IGF-1 to its assistant.

As the name suggests, an insulin-like growth factor is similar to insulin. However, insulin is secreted by the pancreas and IGF-1 by the liver[16]. They work similarly but are activated during different processes. This description is crucial as it will help you understand IF even more.

And now for something very important! When we need energy and have insulin reserves in our veins, insulin will utilise sugar to provide energy. However, when we do not eat - for example during IF - IGF-1 will draw energy from our stored fat.

Therefore, insulin works when you eat, and IGF-1 when you do not. We can get the positive effects presented in this book with thanks to periods of fasting. The list of these advantages is very long, and some of them have already been discussed, but here is a reminder of what they will include: building muscle mass and increasing muscle efficiency, a stronger heart, faster wound healing, and fat reduction.

In addition, IF has a positive effect on bone structure. It protects against osteoporosis, improves blood sugar regulation, and lowers the risk of developing diabetes. Changes in eating style protect against dementia, neurological diseases and has a positive effect on our skin. It is worth looking at the long list of positive effects mentioned by Jillian Levy. You can find a lot of information from her, including relevant studies[13].

Although IF is widely recognised as a weapon against the formation of cancer cells (mainly by keeping insulin levels low and increasing processes within autophagy), it is not fully known if it will impact ill individuals in a harmful way. IGF-1 is responsible for cell growth - this applies to all cells, unfortunately. If a person already has cancer, i.e., there are cancer cells in their body, IGF-1 will lead to the rapid growth of these cells in some types of cancer. IGF-1 itself does not cause cancer, but it can cause rapid growth of an existing disease[21]. On the other hand, it can have a positive effect during chemotherapy.

The most prominent personality in the field of IGF-1 research is Professor Valter Longo. He has researched IF and chemotherapy. He found that IF protects healthy cells from the harmful effects of chemotherapy, but does not protect cancer cells[22]. Another research study showed that fasting increased the effects of chemotherapy in certain types of cancer[61].

The professor himself conducts regular IF and applies 4-days of fasting every six months, during which he drinks only water. In his research, professor Longo proves that our bodies go into a restorative, regenerative state whenever we are deprived of food, even for a relatively short fast. The body slows down its processes to survive the fasting period until food is provided again. Unfortunately, cancer cells are governed by different rules.

Insulin - the hormone that makes you fat?

Many people reading the above subtitle may be outraged that we gain weight from a caloric surplus. Of course, these people are correct. After reading this chapter, however, you will understand that this may not be the whole truth. Let's start by explaining what insulin is and try to figure out what it is all about.

Insulin is a hormone produced by the pancreas, an organ located on the left side of the body, under the lower ribs. The primary and most important function of insulin is to lower blood glucose levels.

A person with an average weight will have around 5 to 6 litres of blood in their body. Due to the difference in body size and weight, men have about a litre of blood more than women. The acceptable blood glucose level is 99 mg/dL, equivalent to about 1 teaspoon of sugar dissolved in a few liters of blood. Anything above this norm is removed by insulin.

Unfortunately, however, an average person eats about 30 teaspoons of sugar each day. According to a Ministry of Health report, each of us consumes more than 40 kilograms a year on average. It is worth reading the full report - its content is frightening.

Consider how much sugar you use for baking, or maybe you feel you already use healthier substitutes? Making a tasty three-banana smoothie? There are three teaspoons of sugar in one banana! Fruit fructose is also sugar!

So, let's get back to the topic of insulin. We already know that it is responsible for lowering blood glucose, but another role of insulin is to allow cells to absorb glucose from the blood. Imagine that insulin works like a key that unlocks a door. Insulin opens this 'door' in the cells to activate the inflow of high-energy glucose.

Another essential function of insulin is the accumulation of glucose in the liver and muscles, in the form of a polysaccharide - glycogen. Knowledge of basic biochemistry will enable you to draw some conclusions on your own and answer any questions about nutrition during IF periods. Understanding these processes will also allow you to comprehend the essence of IF better.

Glycogen is stored in the liver and muscles and is the energy source that is quickly available to the body. Any excess glycogen is stored as fat, because insulin contributes to the storage of adipose tissue - causing you to gain weight simultaneously. In this sense, insulin is the hormone that promotes excess weight under the condition that we provide our bodies with excess sugar from food. It is crucial to be aware that fat can also accumulate on our internal organs.

It is now time to mention insulin's function, which is essential in our efforts to lose weight. Here is something that we should keep in mind: insulin blocks fat burning. After consuming a high-carbohydrate meal, insulin causes not only glycogen deposition but also sodium retention in the tissues. These two mechanisms result in water retention in the body. So, if you eat sweets, chances are you will retain water too. But if you give up sweet things, after a short while you will then start to notice a rapid weight loss. Your body gets rid of the excess water because you have successfully regulated your insulin level. The inflammation in the body caused by high blood glucose levels will also subside.

However, if you are an overeater, consuming high amounts of sugar a day, you will lead yourself to a state where your insulin will no longer be able to cope.

You may be thinking to yourself - what does that mean, 'unable to cope'? Well, if insulin has already deposited significant glycogen reserves in to the liver and accumulated kilograms of fat, and you continue to eat sweets and drink tea with a few teaspoons of sugar, the key that previously opened the door to the cells stops working properly. It is a state referred to as insulin resistance.

When the pancreas can no longer produce enough insulin, it causes a condition called type II diabetes. The 'key' no longer works, which makes blood glucose rise - and because the door is now unable to open, your cells can't access it. The body's cells will continue to send a signal to the pancreas, asking for more insulin, but the door to the cell will not open.

This means that we feel like eating something sweet. Some people are constantly craving sweets, and the reason is because of the processes described. Therefore, if you are classed as overweight and you feel the urge to eat sweets constantly, consider this explanation.

In his bestseller, Michael Moseley, MD, wrote that we must limit simple carbohydrates and instead enrich the diet with fats and vegetables to stop this inevitable path to diabetes. Such a change will not cause large fluctuations in insulin in our blood[19]. Moseley points out that IF may be an effective tool in the fight against insulin resistance, or type II diabetes.

In his book, Moseley describes an experiment carried out by scientists in 2005. The participants of this experiment were asked to eat without a caloric deficit so that they would not lose weight. They were told to eat within a 4-hour eating window. After just two weeks of IF, it was found that insulin sensitivity was significantly better, which may improve the ability to burn fat as a result. Moseley admits that since he started using IF, his blood glucose levels have improved significantly.

Now let's talk a little more about what improves insulin sensitivity and what causes its undesirable increase. Eric Berg excellently describes the behaviour of insulin during IF.

High protein levels can trigger an undesirable rise of this hormone, and the combination of sugar and protein will aggravate this phenomenon even further. Berg does not recommend consuming more than 170 grams of protein per meal.

The very act of eating triggers the production of digestive enzymes, which in turn influences insulin secretion. Stress also affects the secretion of cortisol into the blood and provokes the release of insulin.

Drinking too much coffee gives the same result. One or two cups are OK, but more significant amounts will release cortisol and, consequently, insulin. Therefore, it's wise to cut down on black coffee during fasting too. Otherwise, insulin will appear in the bloodstream.

Berg claims that apple cider vinegar will have a positive and desirable effect on insulin - and its consumption is allowed during IF. Also, products rich in potassium and chromium will affect insulin sensitivity positively. These products should be eaten within eating windows.

Finally, I must mention the theory and practice of Jason Fung, MD, a nephrologist by training, who has been specialising in the treatment of insulin resistance and type II diabetes using IF.

In one of his interviews, Fung gives hope to diabetic people, stating that type II diabetes is reversible to a certain extent[20]. He also wants everyone to know that diabetes is not a disease that has to keep getting worse. He mentions that it is customary in the medical community to tell patients that diabetes is a chronic disease. Thus, it is understood by the general public as an incurable condition that lasts a lifetime.

Fung believes that type II diabetes is caused by insulin resistance, making it reversible. In his publications, he discusses the significant influence IF has in the treatment of diabetes.

I should mention here that Fung's work is promising in terms of treating diabetes through employing IF, because he is a medical doctor with experience of treating patients.

It was Fung who said that we gain weight because of insulin, not just excess calories. He feels that we would not have to worry about overeating if our diet did not contain simple carbohydrates. Our bodies would not crave food so much, and therefore we would not exceed the required number of calories we need. All due to the lack of spikes in insulin concentration and the fact that the body would start taking energy from fat, and not stored glycogen.

Of course, if it was only that easy... IF works because we allow our bodies to draw energy from stored fats. So, you may round up your own conclusions on weight loss from the evidence given.

The glycaemic index is only half the truth!

When researching into the glycaemic index, you may view it as a tool to avoid large fluctuations in glucose levels in the body. After all, some diets are mainly based on the low glycaemic index (GI).

You can see information regarding this on many food products. The glycaemic index measures how quickly your blood sugar rises after you eat a specific carbohydrate. This index is presented on a scale from 1 to 100. You may have guessed correctly that the GI 100 index is, of course, glucose - which is one of the carbohydrates.

Of all macronutrients, only carbohydrates have a glycaemic index. Meat or cheese do not have a GI because they are not carbohydrates. Foods with a high GI index are absorbed in the body and raise blood sugar rapidly.

By consuming food products or meals with a high GI, we lead to postprandial hyperglycaemia. During hyperglycaemia, there is a rapid release of glucose into the blood, which in the final stage causes the sugar to drop below its initial level. Consequently, we feel like eating again and again. It is like a vicious circle, making losing weight even more difficult, especially so for people with obesity and insulin resistance. Low GI foods, on the other hand, are digested more slowly and enter the bloodstream gradually.

It might seem that the knowledge of GI helps us to make a groundbreaking discovery in the field of healthy nutrition.

Unfortunately, the truth is more complicated, and the GI tells only the partial truth. There is something else to be aware of, called Glycaemic Load (GL).

The carbohydrates that we consume have a glycaemic index and a glycaemic load. The glycaemic load is the content of carbohydrates in carbohydrate products. Sounds weird, right? It's like someone discussing the content of 'tomato' in a tomato! Though it sounds strange, the way specific foods affect blood sugar depends on the GI and the number of carbohydrates in that food.

Now a quick question: Which fruit will cause higher hyperglycaemia, or make us feel like eating more? To make answering the question easier, here are the GI values for a banana and watermelon. GI for a banana = 72; IG for a watermelon = 75

Possible answers:
A: A banana
B: A watermelon
C: Both will have the same effect

Correct answer: a banana.

Although bananas have almost the same glycaemic index as watermelons, they differ in terms of glycaemic load. Bananas are high in carbohydrates, which increases blood glucose and, therefore, an aggressive secretion of insulin that may lead to an increase in our appetite. Watermelons, which also have a high glycaemic index, have an amount of carbohydrates which is much lower than bananas.

It also matters whether we eat a banana alone or combine it with protein or healthy fat. For example, we can add it to yogurt, or eat it in an avocado salad. It also matters whether we eat the yogurt or avocado first, and then the banana.

When using IF, after many hours of fasting you should think carefully about your first meal. Ask yourself: is it wise to eat quickly digestible carbohydrates, especially if you're hungry? Does cereal with a high sugar level and a sliced banana still sound like a good breakfast option, or more like a pudding?

Whatever choice we make, we will start to be more aware and make sense of nutritional aspects over time.

Uncontrollable hunger: Are hormones to blame? And what does the Paleolithic period have to do with all of this?

Many of you have years of attempted weight loss behind you. The experience of unsuccessful attempts to lose weight for decades can dishearten some people. Most then look for a radical change in their eating habits, that will alter how they think about diets and health forever.

What is so problematic about this? Why do we have such a problem with obesity nowadays? Does our strong will matter or do hormones regulate everything?

Unfortunately, even science has no definite answers to these problems. Otherwise, by this day and age we could probably go shopping and simply buy a pill to lose weight.

Although there are no clear answers from the world of science, there are already some concrete facts, and it is vital to understand them. To clarify this topic, we should first go back several million years in time, namely to the Paleolithic age. So, what interesting events took place in the Old Stone Age? What does it have to do with IF, anyway?

Firstly, let's look at the primitive people and their lifestyle. They obtained food by hunting and collecting edible parts of plants[23]. Towards the end of the Paleolithic, the ancestors of modern humans replaced the hunter-gatherer way of life with agriculture – though, obviously, there were no tractors or combines back then.

As you probably know, we have not changed genetically since then. So, let's consider what has changed. Primitive men couldn't just take out cereal from the pantry, or make sandwiches with

white bread. No, they had to run and walk for hours just to find some wild berries to enjoy breakfast. So, we can say that by Intermittent Fasting, it is the modern world's way of attempting to live by our early nature.

Wikipedia states that: "About 65-70% of the food eaten by humans during the Paleolithic period was made up of unprocessed fruit, pulses, nuts, and other plants besides grains. The rest of the food eaten by primitive humans came from animals."

Supposing we have not changed genetically since the Paleolithic, why have we wandered so far from our nature? Unfortunately, it is due to the modern diet and lifestyle, which are not adapted to the body's needs in the same way the Paleolithic lifestyle was.

In those days, our body clearly told us when to eat and when to accumulate the fat necessary for survival. Leptin is the hormone that plays a crucial role in this mechanism. We should also be aware of at least two other hormones, namely insulin, which we have already elaborated on, and ghrelin.

Without a doubt, everyone knows the feeling of a gurgling stomach. This is caused by ghrelin. When our belly is empty, it starts to secrete ghrelin, which conveys a message to the brain: "I'm hungry, feed me!".

Mindy Pelz explains that the best way to stay full for a long time and thus reduce the hunger signal to the brain is to eat meals high in protein and fats. Simple carbohydrates, such as white bread or white pasta, are quite the opposite, as they digest quickly, and you feel hungry again in a relatively short time. It is imperative to understand these basics. Without them, we will keep making the same mistakes - constantly and unseccessfully attempring to lose wight due to inability to control hunger

Another significant hormone is leptin, which is contained in fat cells. When released into the bloodstream, leptin carries a message to the brain that reads, "Stop eating, I'm full!" The concentration of leptin depends on the level of fat in your body.

Following that reasoning, we can state that a lot of leptin in our system should be associated with bombarding our brain with messages like, “Hey! My friend! I'm already full! Put away the food - stop eating!” However, as many of us know, it does not seem to work that way. On the contrary, many of you can say that when you start to eat, you cannot stop because you still feel the urge to eat more.

In this regard, multiple questions arise. Why can't I stop eating once I start? Why am I gaining weight? After all, I eat so little! The answer to these questions may be leptin resistance.

We have already touched on the subject of insulin resistance. Remember my comparison in the previous chapter on insulin? I compared cell receptors to a kind of door then. Just like insulin resistance, our hormone receptors also ‘close their doors’ in the case of leptin resistance. If we are overweight, there is so much leptin in our bloodstream that our receptors no longer respond to the messages we send. Therefore, some people feel constantly hungry.

Eric Berg believes that the best way to regulate leptin is to increase the amount of fat in your diet and lower your insulin level. How can you do that? The solution is simple - it is enough to limit simple carbohydrates in your diet.

Just recall the Paleolithic people and what they used to eat. Try to eliminate simple carbohydrates and eat more healthy fats instead. These include avocado, eggs (the yolks are the fat), and olive oil. Enjoy protein and fat dishes for breakfast and see how long you will be full and satisfied. I have included ideas for protein and fat meals later in this book.

On his YouTube channel ‘Dietary Motivator’ (Motywator Dietetyczny), Damian Wiatrowski perfectly presents hormonal relationships, and how protein and fat breakfasts positively affect hormonal balance. In one video he discusses a study conducted by scientists: One group of volunteers ate meals high in protein and fat - in contrast, the second group enjoyed a bagel with ham and tomato. The calorific value of both meals was the same[24].

Damian explains that an optimal hormonal configuration characterised the blood count and saliva of the group consuming more fatty meals. On the other hand, the blood count of the group consuming the bagel was not as good since there were cases of so-called postprandial hyperglycaemia. If you recall, I mentioned postprandial hyperglycaemia in the previous chapter.

It should be noted that IF helps to regulate hunger. This diet brings us closer to the Paleolithic people who did not have the modern problem of obesity. Additionally, they had to try hard to get food, which resulted in them not eating for hours or even days. Compare this with the modern person, whose food is readily available, which in turn causes problems with metabolism.

Moreover, instead of using up our fat reserves during the winter seasons, our fridge is filled with even more treats. As a result, many people never get to the point when these reserves are depleted.

Some individuals claim that diets do not have the desired effect simply due to the person who wants to lose weight. For instance, some people blame it on their lack of willpower. Others may say, 'I could do it, so you can do it too.' But is this true? The text above clearly suggests that it will be easier for a slim person with relatively well-developed muscle tissue to cope with the feeling of hunger rather than an individual who is significantly overweight.

Also, is it entirely true that an obese person is likely to experience more significant problems with leptin? And is leptin resistance only observed in people with excess weight or big bellies? Not at all - because a seemingly slim-looking person who has low muscle mass may also have this problem. The English language describes such people as 'skinny-fat'. Although they appear to be completely healthy, these people can suffer from endocrine disorders, including leptin resistance.

So, it's essential to move and exercise as much as possible, and for the skinny-fat, strength training may be a good option. Mindy Pelz's advice is to first focus on regulating the hormones mentioned above through good nutrition and food products rich in healthy fat and protein. Otherwise, the caloric deficit itself may not be as effective. The lost calories will quickly find their way back if we do not follow healthy eating rules.

Preparatory period for Intermittent Fasting. Fighting the tiger in the 21st century?

A critical but often neglected phase of IF is the process of preparing for the diet. An inadequate approach in the initial stages can do more harm than good. As we know - any starvation diet, fasting, or training is a great stress for the body. In addition, there are factors such as stress at work, home, and other unforeseen random circumstances.

To explain why this is so important, let's start with what happens in our body under stress, and let's even go back to the basics of our primitive existence.

During the Paleolithic period, we were very poorly equipped when it came to weapons. We could only count on ourselves - our arms and legs, and our friends. When we saw a tiger or any other wild animal, we did not stop to wonder, "Hmmm... Should I run or not?". Before any thought even entered our mind, we were not there anymore - thanks to the "fight or flight" response. Sometimes we would also experience the "Freeze" reaction.

Unfortunately, nowadays, our "tiger" has become stressful work, family problems, or scarce finances. We constantly feel stress, and the "fight or flight" reaction is still our bodies response to these stresses. The moment we perceive a threat, our sympathetic nervous system causes adrenaline to circulate in the blood. This hormone makes the heart begin to beat faster. Our blood pressure and blood glucose levels increase, and the blood becomes more coagulable. Also, the functioning of the digestive and immune systems is temporarily suppressed.

The point is that despite the passage of millions of years, our bodies are always prepared to fight the tiger. This process is fundamental in losing weight. It causes the effect of any diet to be thwarted. When our bodies need a sudden surge of energy to escape the tiger, it utilises glucose from the liver and muscles, and releases it into our bloodstream.

Consequently, this means that our blood sugar rises, similarly to when we have a meal high in carbohydrates. Not only does its level increase, but insulin is released, and suddenly we are hungry. If the stress is powerful, our hands may even shake, and our heads ache. The reason is that the glucose level in the body has dropped below normal. Did your friend get on your nerves? Did your boss tell you off? Did something else bad happen? You can eat the healthiest food in the world, but the constant stress can lead to fat deposits at the sides of your waist.

Scientific research proves that insulin resistance may develop under chronic stress[31]. We should explore the roots of the epidemic of obesity, insulin resistance, or even diabetes. Are only sugar and incorrect eating habits responsible for them? Large-scale research has already confirmed that insulin resistance can be triggered by psychological stress[32].

In today's world, you and your boss can both be responsible for your success in losing weight. This isn't a joke! Creating a positive work environment is extremely important in this process. Perhaps starting your workday with a five-minute group meditation would not go amiss.

In fact, I could write a separate, very extensive book on the effects of stress on our weight and metabolic problems. At this point, however, it is about your awareness and understanding of these processes. We should keep in mind that good sleep and relaxation techniques are fundamental when it comes to losing weight.

A good laugh and a long sleep
are the best cures
in the doctor's book
An Irish proverb

A good thing to consider is becoming more mindful. Think about what happens to you after fighting the tiger. Notice when you are hungry or when you do not feel like eating. And most importantly, think about methods that will help you fight stress. An excellent strategy is mindfulness, or mindfulness training, which we will investigate later in this book.

When the threat is gone, our parasympathetic nervous system should reverse the way we feel and induce a feeling of relaxation by easing the previously tense muscles. However, this is not always the case, because long-term stress can keep our bodies in the 'danger zone'. This means that after a traumatic experience, we cannot relax because the body is still alert. Unfortunately, this harms our digestive system and the immune system and may lead to increased susceptibility to diseases.
IF is highly effective in lowering blood glucose, regulating insulin, or reducing inflammation. Still, it cannot lower the stress hormones in our bodies. Therefore, it is important to follow a few essential tips:

1. Lower your consumption of simple carbohydrates.
2. Do not throw yourself in at the deep end.
3. Provide enough nutrient food.
4. Limit your coffee consumption.
5. Drink plenty of water.
6. Sleep well.
7. Use relaxation - Mindfulness, yoga, walking.
8. Make sure that you have good levels of vitamins and minerals, especially sodium, potassium, and magnesium.

How many meals do we eat during IF? The 16:8 method

Scientific research suggests that an average person eats 15 hours a day, which is most of the day. People often do not realise that a snack such as a packet of crisps or some fruit is also a meal. Therefore, you need to consider your current eating style.

When do you start and finish eating? What do you eat? It could be helpful to write it down together with a date to understand your starting point. Doing this will make it possible for you to look at your notes in a few months and see how far you have come and feel proud of yourself.

You should eat no more than 3 meals during IF. However, if you have been eating 5-6 meals on average, it is best to minimise this number gradually. You can try to decrease the number of meals by 1 meal a week, but if you find this too difficult, you can do it more slowly over time.

You should monitor your body and even use a blood glucose meter, if possible, to check your blood glucose - especially if you suspect metabolic problems. People with diabetes or insulin resistance ought to consult their GP or dietitian.

Once you start to control your hunger effectively with 3 meals a day, you can think about reducing this number to two or even one meal (OMAD), if that is your goal, of course. I should emphasise that the shorter the eating window and the fewer meals, the more time you have to think about what you will eat and pay attention to the nutritional value of your meals.

As I mentioned before, some IF practitioners will naturally and quickly move to 2-3 meals, while others may need a little more time to adjust. Just think about our Palaeolithic ancestors who did not have refrigerators or freezers - eating 5-6 meals per day is not consistent with our nature. On the other hand, today we are used to eating all the time, so we will need time to adapt.

Lower your intake of simple carbohydrates

Before you try IF and start reducing the number of meals you eat, as well as the time in which you eat them, lower your intake of simple carbohydrates. Of course, I mentioned earlier that IF does not impose on us what to eat. However, to effectively reduce the number of meals consumed during the day, it's helpful to initially follow this step.

The source of simple carbohydrates is sugar (both white and brown!), honey, fruit types with a very high sugar content (grapes, ripe bananas), as well as highly processed products (sweets, breakfast cereals, sweet pastries). The point here is not that you must completely exclude these products, but consciously minimise their amount in your diet. This action will help you to control your hunger during IF better.

This is especially important for people who are used to snacking throughout the day, and whose diet consists primarily of simple carbohydrates. If you do not lower their amount in your diet and begin the reduction of the number of meals straight away, you may experience headaches and even hand tremors. Many people throw themselves in at the deep end and then cannot control their hunger. Their hands shake, or they get dizzy. It is better to take small steps rather than a big step that may discourage you unnecessarily.

Occupy yourself with something and be active

Instead of looking at your watch all the time and thinking about your food - do something! Clean your house, go for a long walk, play with your kids, or wash the car. Do whatever you want to do to not think about eating. The beginnings are always tough, but soon you will see how quickly you are able to adapt.

Don't let temptation get the better of you - think your meals through!

At the very beginning of using IF, you may feel severely hungry, but do your best to plan your meals for the next day with this new limited number of meals. Acting without a plan can expose you to impulsive consumption of whatever you get your hands on, and we want to prevent that.

It is also essential to take your food with you to work rather than buy readily available and simple carbohydrate foods. If you are going on a business meeting or trip, take some easy-to-store products with you. This could be various types of nuts or fruit - avocado, kiwi, or oranges. Once you have adjusted to this approach, you will notice its advantages, especially when travelling.

Drink a lot of water!

There are many reasons why you should drink plenty of water. Drinking water during your fasting hours will help you control your hunger and keep your body hydrated. Water, which stimulates the kidneys, helps to detoxify our bodies. We tend to confuse feeling hungry for being thirsty, so drink water first if you think you are hungry. It is recommended to drink about 2.5 litres of water a day.

If you do not like the taste of plain water, add some mint leaves or a lemon slice. You can also drink sparkling water. It might be an excellent idea to get a cool water bottle - there is a wide range of water bottles in shops. Take your bottle to work, the gym, or your car - always have it at hand.

Some water bottles have hours and lines drawn on them so that you know how much and when you need to drink. You can also install a phone application that will remind you to drink water.

It is also advisable to introduce good drinking habits in your household. You can, for example, compete with your children to find out who drinks their water faster. This way, both you and your family members benefit a lot because you motivate each other.

What if the fasting period is less than 16 hours?

A 16-hour fast may be easy for some people – something they don't find difficult to do. For others, it can be a source of stress - psychological, but also physical. Therefore, some people may be tempted to fast for less than 16 hours. But is this effective? I am sure you have your opinion on this after reading the chapter devoted to the physiology of IF. The answer is: "Yes, it is, 'but'..."

We will discuss that 'but' in more detail. You can fast for a shorter time, but as you have read before, you will not achieve a sufficient level of autophagy, which takes 17-24 hours to be optimal. Of course, in the case of people on a low-carbohydrate or ketogenic diet, these processes may occur earlier. Why is that? Well, the glycogen stored in the liver will not be as high as in a person who eats a lot of simple carbohydrates.

Therefore, it would help if you gave thought to the content of simple carbohydrates in your diet, especially when you are not yet ready for the entire 16 hours of fasting.

Keep in mind that only after 12-13 hours we start to reap the benefits of IF, due to the growth hormone. After about 13-15 hours, glycogen levels are depleted, and we begin to draw energy from fat. If we add a low-carbohydrate or ketogenic diet with exercise, even 13 hours of fasting will be effective. The exercises that I mentioned earlier in the chapter on IF physiology include strength exercises, intervals, and even jumping on a trampoline.

In my group dedicated to IF, I conducted a survey where women and men could vote on the number of fasting hours they use. The group consists of several thousand people, with 92% of them being women. The survey showed that out of 176 male and female voters:

126 members fast for 16 hours - 122 women and 4 men
21 fast for 20 hours - 18 women and 3 men
11 members fast for 18 hours - 9 women and 2 men
5 members have only one meal a day - only women
4 members pick the combination of the 5:2 method and the 16:8 method - only women
4 members fast for 14 hours - only women
(data from July 25, 2019).

While the above results are impressive, let us remember that Rome was not built in a day. Many of the respondents started with shorter fasting periods, gradually accustoming their bodies to longer periods.

What can you drink during IF?

Point 1.

Only water, preferably spring or mineral water, is allowed to achieve optimal results without compromise.

Drinking water only constitutes the most advanced IF level. Alternatively, you can add a little sea salt or Himalayan salt to your water in order to be able to replenish your electrolytes.

You can also check water composition and choose one with a mineral content of more than 500 mg/l. You can drink sparkling water if you like.

Point 2.

Slight deviations are allowed so as not to go crazy:

- black coffee
- black tea
- red tea
- green tea without additives (you can use jasmine)

- herbal tea
- earl grey (no additives)
- water with a little lemon juice (a slice or two)
- water with apple cider vinegar
- water with a bit of fresh ginger (for flavour)
- water with freshly picked mint

Do not drink:

- fruit tea
- chicory coffee
- yerba mate
- beverages with sweeteners, especially stevia and aspartame
- alcohol
- coffee or tea with milk
- bulletproof coffee
- drinks with any sugar
- coconut water

I would say that this is an intermediate level of difficulty during IF. You will still achieve or maintain autophagy and ketosis. You will also get turbo fat burning, and your growth hormone will be released into the bloodstream.

Point 3.

A few words for beginners who cannot live without milk in their coffee:

If you think IF is something you want to implement in your life, but you cannot imagine your day without a little milk or sweetener in your coffee, you can still try it.

Give yourself some time, a week or even a few, to adjust while you continue to add milk or sweetener to your favourite drinks. Then, try to reduce the amount gradually. Your body will certainly get used to drinking drinks without these additives over time.

Another good solution is to replace cow's milk with unsweetened almond milk.

The mere act of limiting the hours of your eating window and the amount you eat during the day will positively affect your body. However, you must remember that adding cow's milk or sweeteners risks disrupting critical processes so much desired by IF users.

Fasting gives our entire digestive system a chance to take a break from constant processing. Our digestive system will not devour our old cells, toxins, or other waste which lives in our bodies. Instead, it will be using the 10 or 20 calories that we provide to it.

Although providing a small number of calories is certainly a compromise for beginners, if you want autophagy and turbo calory burning, consider points 1 and 2 only. Good luck!

I also encourage all beginners to visit our Facebook support group, which is an invaluable treasure trove of knowledge.

What do the members of our Facebook Intermittent Fasting group drink?

In the survey conducted on August 19, 2019, in the "Intermittent Fasting 16:8 - Poland - Intermittent fasting - 8-hour diet" group, over 220 people voted on the liquids they drink most willingly during IF.

Unsurprisingly, the most popular liquid was water. Here are the top five beverages among the members of the group:

1. Water
2. Black coffee
3. Herbal tea
4. Water with lemon
5. Black tea

I have mentioned water before. But what about that little black coffee that came in second?

Black coffee

We can drink black coffee during fasting. There are 5 calories in one cup of 250 ml. However, it should be remembered that coffee containing caffeine in large amounts may thwart our fasting period.
This is because caffeine affects our adrenal glands, which can lead to the secretion of cortisol and, consequently, stimulate insulin secretion. A cup or two of black coffee with caffeine during fasting is acceptable, but you should not drink more.

Bone broth is different from regular broth

I was wondering for a while if I should mention bone broth.

However, I ultimately decided not to put it on any list because opinions among IF gurus on this subject differ. Some of them believe you can drink it, while others disagree.

Eric Berg claims that bone broth constitutes an excellent replenishment of electrolytes for the body during long fasting periods[50]. Jason Fung also recommends it during fasting[51].

On the other hand, Thomas DeLouer, a personal trainer known amongst the world of American celebrities, states that bone broth disrupts fasting because it has a caloric value, and it is difficult not to agree with this claim[52].

Therefore, in this case, I also encourage you to self-test on a glucometer if you want to drink bone broth during your fasting.

Does a sweet taste in your mouth mean your fasting has been disrupted? Chewing gum ZERO, sweeteners, Cola ZERO

Opinions on whether you can eat sweet-tasting products with ZERO calories are divided and ambiguous. Each person is different and reacts slightly differently to various types of sweeteners. I feel that if you really like to drink something and you want to be sure that it will not increase your blood glucose, you should do a blood glucose test.

Let's look at two scientific studies on this matter and try to arrive at a conclusion. Due to the ambiguity of these scientific studies, I included the aforementioned products in the group of prohibited ones.

So, let's analyse a 2008 study conducted on humans which aimed to investigate whether different types of flavours affect insulin secretion[33]:

During the fasting phase, healthy volunteers rinsed their mouths

(without swallowing) with fluids of eight different flavors. They did this with each liquid for 45 seconds and spat the liquid out without swallowing it. Each flavor was tested on different days.

Blood was drawn each time to check the concentration of glucose and insulin in the blood serum. The concentrations were tested 3 minutes before and 3, 5, 7, and 10 minutes after tasting a specific liquid.

It was concluded that a significant increase in the concentration of sucrose and saccharin in the blood serum occurred after the participants tasted the sweet liquid. Furthermore, scientists stated that both sucrose and saccharin activate insulin secretion, even if the mouth was only rinsed with the mixture.

Another study from 2007 was conducted on rats. This study tested the effect of sweet taste on the blood insulin levels of these animals. It also showed that sweet taste induced an increase in insulin levels.

In the same study, but during its second stage, scientists cut off the nerve connection so that the rats could not taste any flavours (poor rats!). When they could no longer taste the flavours, they were given the sweet substance again, but this time the insulin levels did not rise.

Therefore, the researchers proved that the sweet taste, not the calories, make hormone levels increase.

How can I calculate it all?

The calculations listed below are not necessary to do during IF. Success in using IF should eliminate the need to do any calculations. However, they may be helpful for some beginners.

Step 1 – Basal metabolic rate

If you are overweight, the first thing you need to know before you start losing weight is your Basal Metabolic Rate (BMR).

What is it? Well, BMR is the energy that your body needs to perform basic physiological functions. It is essential, among other things, for breathing, the operation of your heart, other organs, and the endocrine system.

There are differences in BMR between women and men, therefore the formula for its calculation is slightly different for each gender. The average BMR for women is about 1,400 calories per day, while it is about 1,800 calories per day for men. You should also keep in mind that there are several formulas for calculating the BMR. Still, none of them are perfect because they do not consider several other important parameters, including muscle mass in relation to body fat.

Obviously, two people weighing the same can differ in the amount of muscle tissue - and people with more muscle mass may need a little more energy. Unfortunately, none of the adopted formulas considers this factor.

Formulas for calculating BMR also do not take into consideration factors such as ambient temperature or body temperature.

Contrary to some myths, we burn more calories in low temperatures, not the other way around. This is because the body needs more energy to regulate its temperature.

The best and probably most accurate BMR formula is the Harris-Benedict equation, presented below. It considers height, weight, age, and gender. It is, therefore, widely used in dietetics.

Formula for women:

BMR = 655 + (9.6 × your weight) + (1.8 × height in cm) – (4,7 × your age)

Example:

BMR = 655 + (9.6 × 70kg) + (1.8 × 164cm) – (4.7 × 35) = 655 + 672 + 295.2 - 164.5 = 1457.7 BMR is approximately **1458** calories.

Put down your calculations below:

BMR = 655 + (9.6 × ……………………….) + (1.8 × ……………………….) – (4.7 × ……………….)

Your BMR =……………………………………

Formula for men:

BMR = 66 + (13.7 × your weight) + (5 × height in cm) – (6.8 × your age)

Example:

BMR = 66 + (13.7 × 80) + (5 × 180cm) – (6.8 × 35) = 66 + 1096 + 900 – 238 = 1824 BMR is **1824** calories

Put down your calculations below:

BMR = 66 + (13.7 × ……………….) + (5 × ……………….) – (6.8 × …………….)

Your BMR =………………………………

Step 2 – Total metabolic rate

Now that you have calculated your BMR, the next step is to calculate your total metabolic rate, or 'TMR'. TMR is the number of calories you need to maintain your current weight, while considering physical activity.

Sedentary lifestyle. If you have a sedentary lifestyle and do not exercise, multiply your BMR by the physical activity ratio of 1.2.

Light physical activity. If you exercise 1-3 times a week, multiply your BMR by the physical activity ratio of 1.375.

Medium physical activity. If you exercise quite vigorously 3-5 times a week, multiply your BMR by the physical activity ratio of 1.55.

High physical activity. If you exercise intensely 6-7 times a week, multiply your BMR by the physical activity ratio of 1.725.

Very high physical activity. If you exercise very intensively 6-7 days a week and you perform physical work, multiply your BMR by the physical activity ratio of 1.9.

Example 1 – BMR = 1458 Physical activity ratio = 1.2
Your BMR × physical activity ratio = TMR (total metabolism rate)
So, for example: 1458 × 1.2 = 1749,6 which gives TMR = 1750 the number of calories you will need to maintain your current weight.

Example 2 – BMR = 1458 *Physical activity ratio* = 1.55
Your BMR × physical activity ratio, so for example: 1458 × 1.55 = 2259.9
which gives TMR = 2260 the number of calories you will need to maintain your current weight.

Put down your BMR ……………… × physical activity ratio ………………… = TMR ………………

The result is the number of calories you will need to maintain your current weight.

Step 3 – Caloric deficit

Now that you know how many calories you need to keep your weight, and your goal is to lose weight, you need to consider your caloric deficit. While IF is a beneficial tool for losing weight, you will still need a slight caloric deficit. If, for example, your total required number of calories is 2,260, you should gradually introduce a caloric deficit. You can start with a 200-400 calorie deficit a day.
The total caloric deficit should be 7,000 calories if you want to lose 1 kg. However, keep in mind that you will notice a more significant weight loss in the first two weeks. The initial increased weight loss occurs due to the loss of water accumulated in the body.

This is because glycogen in the body binds water - 1g of glycogen can bind about 3g of water. With the introduction of a healthier diet, limited in simple carbohydrates, we lose the water originally retained by a high glycogen level. In addition, we can observe a reduction in salt and, paradoxically, an increase in fluid intake.

During IF, the levels of insulin, leptin, and other hormones are regulated, which positively affects the weight loss process. The regulation processes take place because you only eat within your eating window.

Do I need to count my calories intake?

The answer is not clear-cut. Some of you do not count calories but eat intuitively and have no problems with your weight. On the other hand, some people do count calories and still gain weight. It is sometimes enough to limit fast food or sweets, and your weight will go down by itself, without the need to count calories.

It is also possible that a person will eat very well, eating plenty of whole food, but they may overestimate the consumed calories. You need to realise that you can eat healthy food, and still gain weight. A frequently consumed portion of nuts or seeds seems to be only a tiny handful, but it may be enough to exceed your caloric balance.

Therefore, it is good to have a benchmark for people who eat well but still find themselves gaining weight. This is where counting calories can be beneficial.

Some people also have an insatiable appetite. They frequently cannot stop eating once they start. IF prevents hormones such as insulin, leptin, or ghrelin from raging in the body, which causes a constant feeling of hunger. It also stops the malabsorption of nutrients.

However, before counting calories, you should consider that sometimes 100 calories in one product is not equal to 100 calories in another product. Sounds weird? Well, 100 calories from a chicken breast and 100 calories from white bread represent the same number of calories but completely different food quality. Thus, calories are not the only thing that matters. The quality of what we eat is also crucial. It is essential to eat as little processed food as possible to get as close as possible to the diet of our Palaeolithic ancestors.

An excellent way to calculate calories is to keep a diary of what we eat. An application on your mobile would be an even better solution. You can try, among many others, **FITATU** or **MyFitnessPal**. These apps help you calculate calories conveniently. In addition, they allow you to calculate macronutrients and your daily required number of calories.

What are macronutrients and do I need to count them?

We hear people talking about "macros" more and more often, and we keep wondering – well, what the hell they are? My secondary school final examination focused on biology, and I have personally completed studies in two fields. Still, when I heard about macros for the first time, it did not occur to me that it referred to proteins, fats, and carbohydrates. My twenty years of weight loss experience suddenly encountered a new era.

I should probably also mention that carbohydrates are often referred to as carbs in colloquial language. Now that I have introduced everyone to the 21st century, it is time to start talking about macros seriously.

As you may know, each of these macronutrients provides calories to our body, but in different amounts. Protein provides 4 calories per gram. The same amount is provided by carbohydrates, while fat provides 9 calories per gram. If you notice 10 g of protein or carbohydrates in the composition of a product, it means that it is equal to 40 calories. On the other hand, 10 g of fat is the equivalent of 90 calories.

Wonderful protein

Proteins are made of small molecules called amino acids, linked together by chemical bonds - just like the beads in a necklace. Amino acids connected in this way build long protein chains, which then form other complex forms.

Our body can produce many of these amino acids on its own, but we need to supply other types with our food. Amino acids that we must provide in the diet and which the body does not produce are called 'exogenous' or 'essential' amino acids because they are necessary for the proper growth and functioning of our bodies[27].

Since we eat only in a relatively short eating window while using IF, it is vital to understand the essence of proteins supplied with our food to plan our meals consciously. This is especially important for people who are physically active. You should remember that IF will protect you against loss of muscle tissue, mainly due to the growth hormone and its anabolic role.

However, I should mention here the first three of the nine essential amino acids: leucine, isoleucine, and valine. They make up about 40% of skeletal muscle mass in the human body, and their primary function is protein biosynthesis. When they appear in the bloodstream, they help build muscle tissue. The three amino acids mentioned above are also known as branched-chain amino acids or 'BCAA'. This name is especially known among physically active people or individuals who do weight training, because BCAA is found in the composition of numerous supplements.

BCAAs are the only amino acids that are not metabolised in the liver. Unlike other essential amino acids, after consumption they go directly into the bloodstream. Consuming even 5 grams of BCAAs causes a substantial increase in insulin. Therefore, BCAAs should not be used during fasting, as they cause a burst of insulin and contain calories - a minimum of 20 calories per serving. Also, there is no need to use supplements because the entire range of essential amino acids can be found in meat, eggs, fish, nuts, seeds, and vegetables.

The process of building muscles does not take place during training, or even several hours after. So, we should pay attention to providing a good level of macronutrients all the time, not just before or after exercising.

The other essential amino acids are phenylalanine, tryptophan, lysine, threonine, methionine, histidine, and arginine. The last two are called 'relatively essential amino acids' because the body produces them - but in insufficient amounts in children and sick people. Animal protein is a complete source of essential amino acids, as animal tissue is very similar to ours.

However, this does not mean that vegetarians and vegans cannot get the essential amino acids from plant proteins. Those of you who do not eat meat or animal products can supply your bodies with these amino acids, but you will need to combine two types of protein in one meal so that it then contains all the essential amino acids.

Protein can be a fantastic weight-loss tool. One of the reasons why it is crucial to keep your protein levels high is that it will keep you fuller for longer than carbs or fat. Hence, we should limit simple carbohydrates in favour of protein. Such a change will help you control your hunger more easily and reduce your caloric needs throughout the day.

There are 4 calories per gram of protein, but you will need 20-30% of its energy to digest it. It is related to the so-called thermic effect of food, i.e., TEF.

Suppose you eat 100 grams of protein during the day - 100 grams times 4 calories for every gram of protein will give you a total of 400 calories. Your body will need at least 80 calories to burn 400 calories from protein, so the caloric balance of 100 grams of protein will not be 400, but 320 or fewer. Taking care of a good level of protein in our diet is therefore essential if we want to lose unnecessary kilograms and thus have the appropriate level of muscle tissue.

When using IF, the first meal after a long period of fasting plays a critical role. Ideally, this meal should contain protein and fat and as few simple carbohydrates as possible. You can probably guess that simple carbohydrates in the first meal will cause insulin to rise. This increase is something we do not want as it could lead to an increased appetite during the day. Scientific research proves that protein increases the feeling of fullness, causing us to eat less during the day, and not to snack[28].

One study was conducted on 19 female volunteers who increased their dietary protein consumption from 15% to 30%. As a result, if protein accounted for 15% of their total caloric needs, the participants increased its consumption to 30% of their total caloric demand[29].

Interestingly, carbohydrates were kept at the same level during the study, i.e., 50% of the diet. Also, fat proportion was reduced from 35% to 20%. It came to light that by increasing the amount of protein in their diet, the participants ate 441 fewer calories during the day. They also lost 5 kg in just 12 weeks. Pretty good results, right?

A further study found that increasing protein in your diet to 25% of total calories decreased cravings by half, as well as reduced thoughts about eating by 60%[30].

So how much protein do we need per day?

The required amount of protein we need depends on many factors, but most importantly on our physical activity level. You can see the recommended dietary allowances (RDA) for protein below. The values refer to adults up to 65 years of age.

Sedentary lifestyle, no physical activity. If you have a sedentary lifestyle and do not exercise, you will need about 0.8 grams of protein per kilogram of your body.
Example:
A person weighing 70 kg. 70 x 0.8 = 56 grams of protein a day.

Moderate physical activity. If you exercise 1-3 times a week, you will need about 1 gram of protein per kilogram of your body.

High physical activity. If you exercise intensely 4-5 times a week, you will need approximately 1.1 - 1.4 grams of protein per kilogram of your body. If you have a sedentary job, but your physical activity is high outside of work, stick to lower values. If you work physically and are also very active after work, stick to the upper values.

Very high physical activity. If you exercise intensively in the gym a few days a week and you do physical work, and you are a woman, stick to the following lower values: 1.5 - 1.8. If you are a man, you do physical work and you do weight exercise, you will need about 1.8 - 2 grams of protein per kilogram of your body.

Before any of this, you need to determine how much protein per day you eat now. If your protein intake is much lower than the recommended value, start gradually increasing it. If you have or have had problems with the kidneys in the past, consult your doctor before increasing the level of protein in your diet.

Body Measurement Tracker

	Date:	Date:	Date:
Neck			
Chest			
Left Arm			
Right Arm			
Waist			
Hips			
Left Thigh			
Right Thigh			
Left Calf			
Right Calf			
Weight			

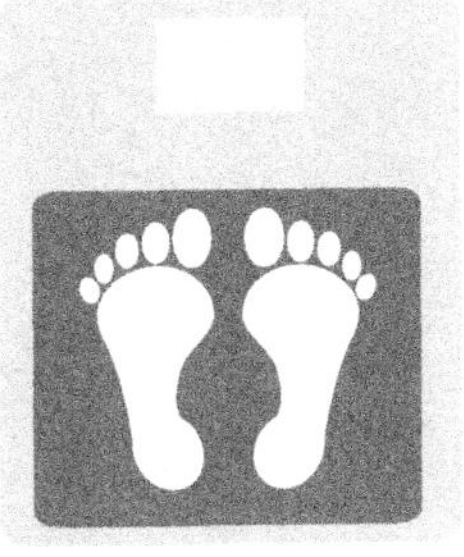

Body Measurement Tracker

	Date:	Date:	Date:
Neck			
Chest			
Left Arm			
Right Arm			
Waist			
Hips			
Left Thigh			
Right Thigh			
Left Calf			
Right Calf			
Weight			

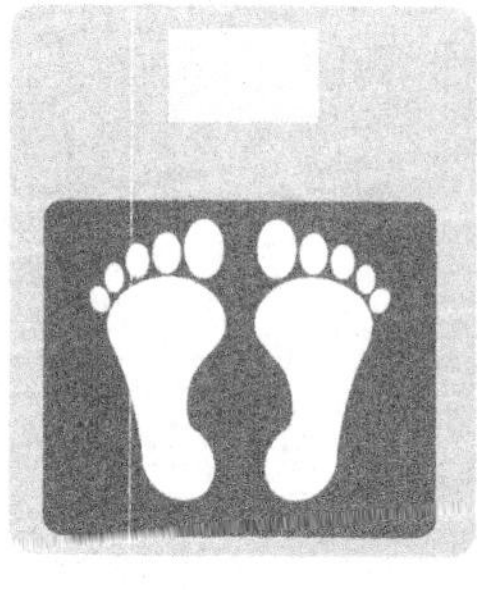

SMART goals - how to wisely achieve your goals.

Setting a goal is an essential element for when we want to lose weight, but also for other aspects of our lives. Whatever goal we want to achieve, it is worth writing down what we want and how we will achieve this on a piece of paper.

Keeping the goal "in your head" without writing it down can turn out to be a dangerous game. We know what we want to achieve, but when our goals start to collide with other, perhaps unforseen life events, we tend to lose sight of our goal. We also often make unrealistic goals for ourselves, for example: "I want to lose 10 kilos in one month." Why not set a goal in a way that maximises your chances of success?

Setting SMART goals will help you increase your chances of achieving them, regardless of whether you want to lose weight, have a six-pack (not only the one you keep in the fridge), or learn a foreign language. The choice is yours! Everything is possible! Be SMART!

SMART is an acronym for:

S – Specific
M – Measurable
A – Achievable
R – Realistic
T – Time-based

SMART GOALS

- ***Specific***

First, think about what exactly you want to achieve. You need to be very clear and specific about your goal. Instead of talking about wanting to improve your general condition, set a specific goal - I want to improve my general condition by jogging three times a week.

- ***Measurable***

It is crucial to be able to measure your goal in some way. Thanks to this, you will see if the goal has already been achieved or what progress you have made. So how can you measure your goal? Well, one way is to use an application to track your journey. It will allow you to control the length, time, and speed of your run. By looking at the history, you can determine how many times you jogged during a given week and how long it took you to run a specific distance.

If you notice that it took you 15 minutes to run a particular distance but now you only need 9 minutes, you will see that you are getting closer to your goal and that your general condition is improving. On the other hand, if your goal is to lose weight, measure the girth of your waist, check your weight, and write down the results in an application or on a piece of paper.

- ***Achievable***

Whenever you set a goal for yourself, it is vital to make it attainable. An ambitious goal, broken down into smaller steps, will be easier to achieve than a huge goal that requires a lot of time.

Bigger goals are often demotivating. Suppose you want to lose 15 kilograms: break down the target weight into two or three smaller ones, for example, 3 goals of 5 kg each.

Every time you reach the next stage of your goal, reward yourself! Go to the cinema with your friends, buy yourself a nice piece of clothing, go to the beautician, do something that will mark the stage of the achieved goal and thank yourself for your hard work. You will be more motivated before moving to the next stage. Little steps will lead you to your bigger goal.

- ***Realistic***

Your goal should be realistic, and you will need to work to achieve your goal. If you feel that you will have a six-pack in a few months, and all you do is sit on the sofa and avoid exercising, your goal is simply a wish, a dream, or a desire... Be realistic!

- ***Time-based***

Set a time frame for achieving your goal. At first, select a small goal and place it in time. By choosing your start and end date, you will take conscious responsibility for what you wish to achieve. If you are about to start your journey with IF and you would like to use this eating style to achieve your weight-loss goals, improve your immunity, or achieve autophagy, you should know that it requires time.

Whatever goal you set, take the time to learn as much as possible about it first. Changing your eating style or habits acquired over the years will also take time. Since your goal is measurable, you will be able to set smaller goals over time.

Let's assume that you are halfway towards your goal, which means that you have already achieved half of your measurable goals. An example can be the goal of losing a pound of weight in a week and a total of 6 kilos (approx. 13 pounds) in 12 weeks. After half the time passes, namely after 6 weeks, you should expect to lose 3 kg (approx. 7 pounds). If you lose more, you will be satisfied and motivated to continue your journey. If you set unreasonable goals, the results will demotivate you to keep going, not to mention the stress that may arise while trying to achieve them.

Take a pen in your hand and carefully plan everything according to the outline above. Do not forget to put the phrase 'SMART goals' at the top of the page.

Remember that S.M.A.R.T. means smart goals and is the only path to success!

Good luck with achieving your goals!
Be SMART

My Smart Goals

1

2

3

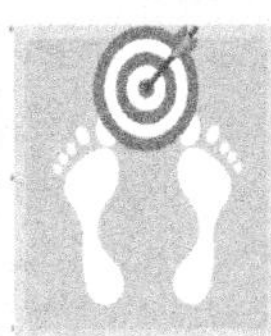

Mindfulness or Mindfulness Training: Break away from the vicious cycle of diets and much more.

We have already mentioned stress in the context of the 'fight with the tiger'. We know that our stress hormone, cortisol, reaches a high level in the early morning hours. We also know why this happens, which is why relaxation techniques are so important in our lives.

As you read this, you can probably think of some ways of calming yourself down that help you during challenging moments. We create mechanisms to cope with emotional stress from an early age. We watched our mums throwing pots out of anger and our dads kicking a sack of potatoes... just kidding! However, the truth is that we deal with stress one way or another, sometimes in a healthy way, sometimes not.

One of the methods that has gained tremendous popularity in recent years is Mindfulness, i.e., Mindfulness Training. It comes from the old Buddhist culture, but it also works perfectly in the modern age.

Mindfulness gives us the ability to stay in the moment. It teaches us to pay attention to one aspect of what we are doing, and we are not supposed to judge whether something is, for example, good or bad, nice or ugly. We simply focus on the moment. Most of us concentrate too much on the future. This means that we try to plan or overthink something, including the consequences of something that has not even happened yet.

Think about the last time you went to the gym or for a run.

Presumably, during the training, you thought about what you would cook for dinner, what homework your child must do at home, whether will you get stuck in traffic for a long time, what your colleague meant at work, or whether you will meet the nice lady or the mean one in the shop on your way back. This happens all the time... Mindfulness is about stopping and being in the moment, at least for a few minutes.

While being at the gym or anywhere else, try to focus only on the activity you are doing at that very moment. Focus your thoughts on what you are doing but try not to judge or criticise.

Concentrate on what you feel in your body or listen intently to music. If you notice any thoughts coming to your mind, just push them away – perhaps imagine that they are little clouds in your head that you can push away. Make sure that you know that the next five minutes are yours: just for you, for your body. Everything else is not important in this moment. Only this moment and being present are what matters.

Mindfulness is a way of observing your thoughts, physical sensations, surrounding sounds, smells, and anything else you would not normally notice. It is a bit like looking at the world through the eyes of a child. When we look at the lawn in the garden, we can see that it has overgrown and the grass needs to be trimmed, while a young child looking at the same lawn may exclaim, "Mummy, look! A spider is walking on the grass!".

Once we are adults, it becomes more and more difficult to see things happening here and now because we are still in the future in our minds. It is just like driving a car. When we initially learn to drive, we pay attention to where the gears and brake are. We wonder what the speed limit is in built-up areas and undeveloped ones.

With time, however, we start to drive better and better, and after many years, if someone asked us what exactly we are doing step by step while driving a car, we would have to think carefully. This is because, at some point, we started to drive on autopilot - automatically and without thinking, sometimes developing bad habits. This 'autopilot' applies to every area of life, including the way we eat.

The constant rush of life means that we often eat on the run. We feel cravings dictated by unstable hormones. We also experience long-time problems with maintaining our weight and make continued attempts to lose weight. We suffer because of years of bad habits, stress, and our hectic lives.

Therefore, it is high time to free ourselves from this chaos. It is time for reflection and change, time for ourselves, being in the present moment, and breaking down habits into smaller units - time for Mindfulness Training. This training applies to every aspect of our lives, and you can start by taking the first step. No criticism, no judgment, no sabotaging thoughts - just being present here and now.

Start with 5 minutes every day. Try breathing techniques, go for a walk, listen to your body, and music - just for a few minutes, be in the present. Using IF helps us be aware of food and ourselves in each moment.

By regulating our insulin levels, we can make informed choices, because we no longer experience hunger urges. IF also allows us to better control the number of macronutrients in our daily diet. We begin to understand and recognise when we feel hungry and when we are full. We can differentiate between thirst and hunger. If you cannot do these things yet, close your eyes for five minutes and listen to your body. Live more consciously and remain in the present moment.

Being in the present will help us train our awareness, but it is not an easy task. Practicing every day, even for 5 minutes, can help us stay focused and fulfil our goals. Otherwise, our minds will be dominated by stressful events and constant fear - we will never be able to enjoy the present moment.

Below I present Mindfulness training that I regularly do with my clients. You may not like every one of them, but you should choose the one(s) that suit you. You will undoubtedly find more ideas on the Internet. Good luck!

Mindfulness training - practice # 1.

Pour warm water into a large plastic bowl, add a few drops of bubble bath. Stir the water with your hand until some foam appears. Dip your feet in the water. Feel the warmth of the water surrounding your feet. Look at the foam and the changing colours of the rainbow. You may hear the air bubbles burst. Can you smell the bubble bath? What do you feel? If you notice any thoughts coming to your head, push them away and slowly return to being present and in the moment. You can close your eyes if you want to, especially if it allows you to be close to this experience.

Mindfulness training - practice # 2.

Sit in a comfortable position in a chair or armchair. You can keep your eyes open or closed. Calmly inhale and exhale. Start counting your inhalations and exhalations in your mind. Keep inhaling and exhaling. Inhale one, exhale one; inhale two, exhale two; inhale three, exhale three, and so on - inhale and exhale until you reach twenty. If you get lost while counting, do not worry. Continue to breathe in and out. If any thoughts appear, simply push them away as if they were little clouds. Move them and throw them away with the eyes of your imagination. Go back to being in the present moment, inhale and exhale.

Mindfulness training – practice # 3.

Take something in your hand; it can be a pen or a mug. Start describing exactly what you can see, but do not judge it by saying that it is old or new, dirty or clean. Just note all the facts: the colours, text, material, all the things that you can see and feel until you run out of options.

I ♡ Intermittent Fasting

You ♡ Intermittent Fasting

He ♡ Intermittent Fasting

She ♡ Intermittent Fasting

We ♡ Intermittent Fasting

You ♡ Intermittent Fasting

They ♡ Intermittent Fasting

Dorota Perkins

High-carbohydrate breakfast ideas vs protein and fat breakfasts ideas.

Once upon a time, there was a Palaeolithic man who woke up and ate a bowl of cereal... just kidding! The Palaeolithic man had to work very hard to eat anything at all. He certainly did not enjoy a high-carbohydrate, high-sugar breakfast.

Stop reading right now. Go to the shelf where you keep your cereal and see how much sugar is in one serving, namely 30 grams. Once you do this, grab 30 grams of cereal and think about whether it is enough for you. Well, it is just a handful, so I doubt it.

An average person will need two or even three portions of this size. How much sugar is in one serving? 7 grams? Multiply 7 times 3. Yes, there is 21 grams of sugar! 21 grams of sugar is as much as 5 teaspoons! Now put 5 teaspoons of sugar on a small plate and try to eat it. Enjoy your meal!

Cereal consists of over 90% simple carbohydrates. The rest is a bit of protein, fibre, vitamins, and an awful lot of good marketing work.

One study devoted to breakfast cereal thoroughly analyzed the products available on the British market and found that the popular Kellogg's Frosties have the highest sugar content among all the products. They contain 4.26 teaspoons of sugar per 30-gram serving! Eating two or three servings is like consuming up to 13 teaspoons of sugar for breakfast. Suppose you are fasting for 16 hours - this amount of sugar can lead to terrible reactive hypoglycemia in some people.

Blood glucose should rise and then gently drop to a lower limit after a well-balanced meal. However, some people develop a pathological reaction called postprandial hypoglycemia. It occurs after meals high in carbohydrates, especially those rich in simple sugars.

In this case, the postprandial glucose concentration rises above the accepted norm but then falls too sharply and excessively. As a result, low sugar level appears, and our body demands food again in a relatively short time.

A person with hypoglycaemia may experience symptoms such as trembling hands, excessive appetite, and headaches. Eating frequent meals with a high glycaemic index can lead to insulin resistance and even diabetes over time.

That is why it is so important to limit simple carbohydrates or sugar in our diet, especially in the first meal after fasting for many hours.

What about a smoothie?

Did the Palaeolithic people have a blender? Hmm...

Which one is easier: drinking 3 blended fruits or eating them whole? How long will it take you to eat 3 oranges, and how long will it take to drink them? What about a smoothie made of 2 bananas, a handful of blueberries with a teaspoon of honey? Sound healthy?

Multiply 12 grams of sugar from one banana by 2, and don't forget about the honey and blueberries. Admittedly, it is an awful lot of vitamins, potassium, and fibre. However, did you think that fructose or honey would not raise your blood glucose just like refined sugar? Of course, they will!

Naturally, no one can forbid you a single banana smoothie, but it may be a wise idea not to add honey to it in the morning.

Smoothies are a good breakfast alternative if they are as low in sugar as possible and contain a good dose of complex carbohydrates.

Any alternatives?

It won't be easy for some people to suddenly switch to breakfasts that are mostly protein and fat after years of consuming high-carbohydrate breakfasts. It should be noted here that for people using IF, breakfast is often eaten no earlier than 10:00 or 11:00. If your first meal has consisted of carbohydrates over the years, it may be good to look at an alternative.

Scientists from Weill Cornell Medical College in New York proved that the order of consumed macronutrients significantly impacts blood glucose levels in overweight people. The volunteers first consumed simple carbohydrates such as ciabatta and orange juice. After 15 minutes, they ate a meal containing protein, fat, and vegetables. Blood glucose levels were checked 30, 60, and 120 minutes after eating.

The following week, the experiment was repeated with the same volunteers. However, this time they ate a meal containing protein, fat, and vegetables first. Next, after 15 minutes, they had ciabatta bread and orange juice. It turned out that when the participants ate protein, fat, and vegetables followed by carbohydrates, the blood glucose level was 29%, 37%, and 17% lower when it was checked after 30, 60, and 120 minutes respectively, compared to the first experiment. The researchers also found that insulin levels were significantly lower when protein was first eaten with fat and vegetables.

The solution?

Consider starting your day with a protein-fat meal with a small number of complex carbohydrates. Such a choice is supported by a wide range of scientific studies on the positive role of protein in the first meal.

Below you can see the protein content of selected products in grams per 100g:

Meat	Grilled chicken breast without skin	32.0
	Grilled beef steak (lean)	31.0
	Lamb (lean)	29.2
	Grilled pork chop	31.6

Fish	Canned tuna in water Grilled mackerel Grilled salmon Grilled cod	23.5 20.8 24.2 20.8
Seafood	Shrimp Clams Crab	22.6 16.7 10.0
Eggs	Chicken eggs	12.5
Dairy produce	Whole milk 3.2% Skim milk 2% Skim milk 1% Cheese (Cheddar) Cottage cheese Full fat yogurt Yogurt	3.3 3.4 3.4 25.4 12.6 5.7 4.8
Vegetable protein	Beans Baked beans Tofu (soy)	6.9 5.2 8.1
	Red lentils Chickpea	7.6 8.4
Grain products	Whole wheat flour Dark bread White bread Cooked rice Oatmeal Cooked pasta	12.6 7.9 7.9 2.6 11.2 6.6
Nuts	Almonds Walnuts Hazelnuts	21.1 14.7 14.1

Poached egg with salmon on a salad mix

***Calories:** 292 **Protein:** 30g **Fat:** 18g **Carbs:** 3g*

Ingredients for 1 serving:

1 egg

2 slices of smoked salmon (approx. 100 g)

a salad mix

vinegar or lemon juice

pepper

black cumin

Preparation

Boil water in a small pot, add a little vinegar or juice from half a lemon. Crack an egg into a small bowl. Reduce the heat and use a spoon to stir the water vigorously and create a vortex. Gently pour in the egg. Keep turning the egg with a spoon until it is tender and cooked – for about 3 minutes. Pull out with a skimmer.

Arrange the salad mix on a plate. Put the slices of salmon on top and then the egg. Season to taste with pepper and sprinkle with black cumin.

Keto bread rolls from 5 seeds

Calories per 1 roll: 230 Protein: 10g Fat: 20g Carbs: 8g

Ingredients for 9 bread rolls:

3 egg whites

310 g of almond flour/ground almonds

2 spoons of baking powder

2 teaspoons of apple cider vinegar or lemon juice

1 cup of hot water

1 teaspoon of sea or Himalayan fine salt

5 tablespoons of ground psyllium seeds (you can grind them yourself)

2 teaspoons of black cumin seeds

2 teaspoons of linseed

½ teaspoon of sesame seeds

½ teaspoon of chia seeds

Preparation

Mix the dry ingredients in a bowl, leaving 1 teaspoon of linseed and 1 teaspoon of black cumin seeds - you will need them to sprinkle the rolls.

Add vinegar (or lemon juice) and hot water to the dry mix in the bowl and mix well. Set aside to cool.

Meanwhile, beat the egg whites until they are quite stiff. Add eggs to the slightly cooled mixture and mix gently.

Preheat the oven to 175 degrees.

Use wet hands to form 9 bread rolls. Place them on baking paper. Sprinkle with the remaining black cumin seeds and linseed. Bake for 50-60 minutes.

The rolls will be ready if you hear a hollow noise when you tap them. The rolls will be fresh the next day. You can also store them in the freezer.

Breakfast muffins with kale and feta - 9 muffins

Calories per 1 muffin: 87 Protein: 6g Fat: 6g Carbs: 2g

Ingredients:

5 eggs

110 g of feta cheese

60 g of kale

½ medium red pepper (approx. 120 g)

chives

pepper

½ teaspoon of olive oil

Preparation

Preheat the oven to 180 degrees. Dice the pepper, feta (65 g), and kale into small cubes (get rid of any tough parts of the kale beforehand). Add the ingredients to a bowl.

Beat the eggs and pour them over the vegetables, season with pepper. Mix everything well. Pour the vegetable and egg mixture into muffin moulds previously greased with oil. Sprinkle the remaining feta cheese on top. Bake for 15 minutes.

Mackerel and egg spread on a salad mix with cherry tomatoes

Calories per 1 serving: 271 *Protein:* 23g *Fat:* 18g *Carbs:* 5g

Ingredients for 3 servings:

170 g of smoked mackerel

4 eggs

76 g of onion

3 tablespoons of Greek yogurt

Cayenne pepper

black pepper

salad - favourite mix

6 cherry tomatoes

Preparation:

Hard-boil the eggs and peel them. Take the mackerel from the skin and bones. Dice the onion into small cubes. Use a food processor to process the eggs and mackerel. Add chopped onion and yogurt to the mackerel-egg mixture and season with a little black pepper. Do not add salt as the mackerel is quite salty. Mix everything well. Put your favourite salad mix and tomatoes on a plate.

----- *Enjoy!* -----

Salad with avocado, green cucumber, and tuna

*Calories per 1 serving: **203** Protein: **10g** Fat: **18g** Carbs: **2g***

Ingredients per 2 servings:

1 avocado (approx. 150 g)

½ Armenian cucumber (approx. 100 g)

60 g of canned tuna without water

1 teaspoon of sesame oil

1 tablespoon of apple cider vinegar

pepper, salt

Preparation:

Peel the avocado and cucumber and then dice them. Add the tuna and seasoning.

Omelette with ham and Philadelphia cream cheese

Calories per 1 serving – an omelette with filling: ***350*** *Protein:* ***24g*** *Fat:* ***20g*** *Carbs:* ***20g***

Ingredients per 1 serving:

Omelette mixture:

2 eggs

1 teaspoon of olive oil or coconut oil

½ teaspoon of herbes de Provence

2 pinches of turmeric

2 pinches of ginger

pepper (no salt)

Filling:

2 slices of chicken ham (approx. 30 g)

1 tablespoon Philadelphia cream cheese (full fat)

1/4 teaspoon pepper spread

½ small red pepper (about 120 g)

lettuce leaves

Extras:

1 heaped tablespoon of natural yoghurt

black cumin

Preparation:

Crack the eggs into a dish, beat them with a fork, and season the mixture according to the ingredients or your own liking.

Put the pan on a low heat and add the oil. The pan should be 18 cm in diameter.

Pour the mixture into the preheated pan. Fry with no lid until the edges of the omelette are cooked. Using a wide spatula, turn the omelette over and fry until the mixture is completely solid.

Mix the pepper spread with the cheese and spread the mix on the cooling omelette. Top with chicken ham, lettuce, and diced pepper.

Fold and cut in half. Serve with yogurt and sprinkle with black cumin.

Smoothie with peanut butter and roasted almonds

***Calories:* 410 *Protein:* 14g *Fat:* 28g *Carbs:* 27g**

Ingredients per 1 serving:

1 flat tablespoon of peanut butter

15 g of roasted almond flakes

½ banana

250 ml of almond milk

1 flat teaspoon of cocoa

a pinch of cinnamon

Preparation

Blend all the ingredients except the almond flakes. Pour the smoothie into a mug and top with roasted almonds.

24-72-hour water fast

It is essential to keep in mind our reasons for doing an extended fasting period. Knowing this will help us stay motivated during the long fasting hours.

The body is an incredibly intelligent system that can use all its energy for detoxification or internal self-repair. This self-healing is clearly visible when we cut ourselves - the body can heal the wound on its own. It is more challenging for us to imagine internal self-healing.

By eating five or six times a day, our body uses a large part of its energy to digest food. This is the reason why IF and occasional longer fasting periods are so important.

Furthermore, the last meal before starting IF shouldn't contain too many simple carbohydrates or a considerable amount of protein, as they can lead to a significant increase in blood glucose, and it will take up to 8-10 hours to regulate its level in the blood.

Therefore, during the 16:8 method, or before long fasts, you should take this fact into consideration. If you do this, the healing processes in our body will begin much faster. As a reminder, I will repeat that the growth hormone, which I wrote about in detail in a previous chapter, begins to be released after about 12 or 13 hours of fasting.

The following process that then take place after 13-15 hours of fasting is our goal. It is then the body switches from taking energy from stored sugar to drawing it from burning our fat. This process can be compared to a fridge-freezer. You have constant access to the fridge, which is a quick source of energy, and the freezer has supplies that we reach for much less frequently. Therefore, in order to start losing fat, you must empty the fridge to begin using your freezer supplies.

When the body begins to take energy from fat, ketone bodies start to appear. The more ketone bodies in your body, the more repair processes occur and the greater the weight loss. Processes connected to autophagy begin after 17-24 hours of fasting. (I wrote about these in detail in an earlier chapter.) Once we reach the 24-hour water fast, we can be sure that the body has started all the processes mentioned above and will continue its miraculous self-healing for up to 72 hours.

I would like to mention here a scientific study by Professor David Sabatini from 2018, which confirmed that after 24 hours of fasting, new intestinal stem cells are produced. Another fascinating phenomenon is the production of the BDNF (brain-derived neurotrophic factor) protein in nerve cells. This protein triggers autophagy processes in our brain.

This process was recognised by Mark Mattson, professor of neurosciences. During this process, our brain's neuroplasticity is improved, and thanks to this our learning and memory abilities improve. Serotonin levels also increase. In the final hours of the 72-hour fast, all these processes are intensified, including the production of stem cells in various parts of the body and rebuilding our immune system.

If you have been using IF 16: 8 or other longer intervals for some time now, you will not have any problems with a 24-hour fasting period. If you use a ketogenic diet with IF, a 24-72-hour fast will be a piece of cake for you. People whose bodies have become used to drawing energy from fat will experience virtually no side effects. If, however, you "live" on simple carbohydrates, I would not recommend jumping into longer fasts without prior preparation, as they entail sudden drops in blood sugar. These drops may result in headaches, hand tremors, and in extreme cases, even fainting. Therefore, I recommend doing extended fasts in stages, using this pattern: 24h → 36h → 72h.

Here is an example of a method for someone who eats during 11 am-7 pm window:

Eat your last meal at the time when you usually end your eating window, e.g., 7 pm. If you are planning a 48-72-hour fast and are not following the ketogenic diet, I recommend that you start fasting on Friday if you have the weekend off. Otherwise, it may be a good idea to take a day off on your second fasting day.

On the second day of water fast, our concentration may be weakened. We may also feel a significant drop in energy. This feeling usually wears off after the second day.

We finish the 24-hour fast after a day - we eat only a 'little something'* for dinner. The next day we return to our regular nutrition and eating window that we used before the extended fast. We start the 36-hour fast on Thursday at 7 pm and end it at 11 am on Saturday. We eat a little something at 11, and then a regular meal after an hour.

We start the 48-hour fast on Thursday at 7 pm, and finish with a small lunch at 7 pm on Saturday. Then we return to our usual eating window and regular eating habits on Sunday between 11 am - 7 pm.

We start the 72-hour fast on Thursday at 7 pm and finish with a little something to eat at 7 pm on Sunday. Then we return to our regular eating window and normal eating habits on Monday between 11 am - 7 pm. In this case, however, I would recommend a small snack like an apple or yogurt at 11 am, and after an hour, a regular, easily digestible meal.

During water fast, we only consume water with the possible addition of Himalayan salt. You should not take any supplements or vitamins because your body will take care of everything. And as always - if we are under the supervision of a specialist doctor, we should consult with them before fasting. Strenuous exercise in the gym should be avoided during water fasting, but light aerobic exercises are allowed.

*A little something - e.g., bone broth or broth, vegetable soup, natural yoghurt, slightly sweet fruit - such as an apple. You should keep in mind that you are lining your intestinal walls again, and therefore you need to eat products that enrich the intestinal bacterial flora.

From Beata's diary

48-hour FAST

Initial weight 53.4kg

Friday 01/11/2019

7:30 pm Last eaten meal.

I ate something fatty to feel full for a longer time. I have been on a ketogenic diet for three months now, so I am used to eating fatty products. I am very motivated and full of hope that I will make it to Sunday, the zero hour. However, I am also considering extending the fast until Monday morning. I will see how I feel then.

Saturday 02/11/2019

07:30 am Woke up. I slept for 8.5 hours.

Feeling good. My water with Himalayan salt is ready, but I must drink coffee. Of course, black with no additives. I guess it is a habit that there must be coffee in the morning. During the fasting period, I decided not to take my hormone medications. Nothing will happen to me without Euthyrox for two days - I think.

11:40 am My usual breakfast time. I am not hungry. So far, I have drunk 1 litre of water.

3:00 pm I am baking a nut cake for my husband and, surprisingly, I can stand the smell very well. I do not feel a drop in energy or any hunger, which is good.

6:00 pm I have noticed that my concentration is slightly lowered.

Sunday 03/11/2019

Slept for 11.5 hours, but the deep sleep phase lasted only 4 hours and 40 minutes. My sleep was rather uneasy, woke up at 4:30. However, I am not sure if this was due to my ongoing fasting or simply related to some family problems that I have.

Besides, I feel good. No feeling of hunger. The perceptible acetone aftertaste that I feel in my mouth is most likely caused by an increased production of ketone bodies.

11:00 am My body is sweating, and I am slightly dizzy. After drinking 1 litre of water with a teaspoon of Himalayan salt, the symptoms disappeared.

Preparing breakfast for my husband did not cause any temptation to try the food. The smell of fried pancakes does not impress me either. Perhaps it is a matter of attitude towards fasting. I do not do it as a punishment, I do it consciously to get effects from autophagy.

2:00-3:00 pm I did my chores without any effort or problems. The whole flat is clean. I still have this acetone taste in my mouth, but I am still not hungry.

5:00 pm I felt cold and had a slight headache until the end of fasting. Apart from that, I felt good. I still did not feel hungry, and my stomach did not growl.

7:30 pm The end of my fast. The first meal was beef bone broth, cooked a day earlier, and a salad mix, cherry tomatoes, radish, cucumber, olive oil, and a tablespoon of apple cider vinegar. Turkey breast with mushrooms and green peas puree with butter. I drank the broth without any problems, but eating solid food was problematic for me because I felt sick at times.

Final weight 52.6 kg.

Circadian rhythms – our biological clocks that cannot be ignored.

In 2017, three American scientists received the Nobel Prize for research related to circadian rhythm. Their discoveries concerned the mechanisms that control the circadian cycle at the molecular level. It sounds complicated; however, the whole idea is relatively easy to understand and fundamental to the basic processes that go on in the body every 24 hours.

Knowing the theory of the circadian cycle is vital when it comes to IF. Knowledge on this subject can help us achieve our weight goals significantly faster and more efficiently. It can also help us understand when to eat our meals and how to maximise the potential of the daily cycle.

The circadian rhythm is a 24-hour biological cycle. It is present in every cell in our body. This cycle is responsible for the daily regulation of physiological processes. As a result, when we sleep, it affects the level of hormones (including insulin) and even our reaction to medication. Our biological clock is in sync with the external environment through exposure to daylight as well as the time when we eat meals[35].

The human body is specifically programmed to go through certain cycles and rhythms throughout the day. Even before we wake up, our internal clock prepares us for it. This process starts with reducing the production of the sleep hormone, namely melatonin. Melatonin is produced by a small endocrine gland called the pineal gland. Our breathing speeds up in the morning; thus, our heartbeat and blood pressure increase, and our body temperature increases by half a degree.

In the morning, a healthy person wakes up refreshed, rested, hungry, and possibly ready to defecate after a night of collecting toxins. The moment we open our eyes, the concentration of cortisol rises, which gives us the energy to start the day before we eat anything else.

Our pancreas starts to become sensitive and super-efficient when it comes to insulin secretion. This condition persists throughout the day with its greatest sensitivity, until noon. Therefore, we should take this into account when preparing the menu for a given day. This is especially true for people who use IF to lose weight.

Eating when the sun is on the horizon is a challenging task nowadays. Many people are at work during these hours, so preparing meals requires military discipline and incredible determination. Our clock in the brain, which regulates all processes in the body, is the most sensitive to light.

The clocks in our internal organs - such as the liver, heart, and kidneys - are most sensitive to food in the first half of the day. Researcher Satchin Panda believes that the first bite of food or sip of coffee in the morning resets the brain and tells the clock in our organs (liver, heart, and kidneys) that it's time to start the day. He claims that changing our routines overnight makes our internal clocks disoriented and confused[36].

In 2015, scientists conducted a study to determine the number of hours and times when people eat. The individuals participating in this study used an application called myCircadianClock. They recorded every meal, snack, or drink using the app. The study found that 50% of respondents ate for 15 hours during the day or more.

Interestingly, people participating in this study who ate for 15 hours, thought that they only ate for 12 hours. It turned out that they did not count their morning coffee with milk, a glass of wine in the evening, or a handful of nuts or crisps as a meal. 25 percent of the respondents ate their first meal two hours later at the weekend.

Scientists dealing with the circadian rhythm maintain that changing mealtimes disrupts our daily cycle. Suppose you are interested in participating in the research carried out by Satchin Panda - in that case, you can install the app mentioned above on your phone, thus contributing to further research in this field. You can also get more information on the circadian rhythm by visiting the website at www.myCircadianClock.org.

More and more publications showing the relationship between the time when we eat food and weight regulation are beginning to appear in the scientific literature. The development of this research on humans progressed significantly after 2017, due to the research on the circadian rhythm being awarded the Nobel Prize.

We are biological beings...
we are not our smartphones,
we are not our computers.
We need to be in touch
with the cycles of nature.

Vincent Pedre, MD

One of the earlier studies comes from 2013[37]. It was supposed to help us to understand the correlation between the time when we consume food and the effectiveness in weight loss. The study was conducted on 420 people who followed a strictly defined regime. All the participants were overweight women at the age of 42 with a BMI of 31. They were divided into two groups.

The first group consisted of women who ate their main meal before 3 p.m. The second group of women ate their main meal late, after 3 p.m. It was concluded that women who ate their main meal earlier experienced a greater weight loss compared to women who ate it later. Caloric consumption was the same in both groups. The researchers stated that we should consider what we eat, and when we eat our meals.

Discoveries concerning biological cycles or internal clocks indicate that the pancreas also has its own clock. Scientists at Northwestern University presented a research study that showed that the pancreatic internal clock regulates insulin production.

If the clock does not work properly, it can lead to diabetes[38]. I had no problems finding many scientific studies confirming this relationship. In a 2013 study, scientists concluded that the circadian rhythm is also disrupted due to the changes in the environment in recent years.

Working shifts, having lights on at night, and lack of sleep play a dominant role in the development of diabetes. Scientists are constantly researching the impact of the circadian cycle on the entire human body[39].
In September 2019, I surveyed the 'Intermittent Fasting 16:8 - Poland - Periodic Fasting - 8-hour diet' Facebook group. The survey regarded the times of meals consumed by the group members using IF. 285 members of the group took part in the survey. It was established that as many as 156 respondents finished their eating window at 7:00 p.m., 129 respondents finished eating after 7:00 p.m., and 92 people at 8:00 p.m.

It was also concluded that the eating window falls within the body-friendly hours of the circadian cycle in most cases. Furthermore, it was found that 239 respondents eat in an 8-hour window, and 36 respondents in a 6-hour window, or a shorter eating window. Finally, 10 people eat within a 10-hour window.

Professor Satchin Panda, who encourages not exceeding
a 12-hour eating window, would be delighted with such results[41].

Here is the detailed information from the survey:

12:00 pm - 8:00 pm = 92 votes; 11:00 am - 7: 00 pm = 54 votes;

9:00 am - 5:00 pm = 26 votes; 10:00 am - 6:00 pm = 23 votes;

8:00 am - 4:00 pm = 17 votes; 10:00 am - 4:00 pm = 15 votes;

1:00 pm - 9:00 pm = 15 votes; 12:00 pm – 6:00 pm = 7 votes;

2:00 pm - 10:00 pm = 6 votes; 4:00 pm - 8:00 pm = 6 votes;

4:00 pm - 10:00 pm = 6 votes; 3:30 pm - 8:30 pm = 4 votes;

12:00 pm - 4:00 pm = 3 votes; 9:00 am - 7:00 pm = 3 votes;

7:00 am - 12:00 pm = 2 votes; 11:00 am - 3:00 pm = 2 votes;

OMAD at 3 pm = 1 vote; 7:00 am - 5:00 pm = 1 vote;

1:00 pm - 7:00 pm = 1 vote; 2:00 pm - 5:00 pm = 1 vote.

Do we already have a recipe for a longevity potion? Sirtuins and Intermittent Fasting.

For centuries, the world has been trying to stop the aging process. The first mentions of such efforts can be found in ancient times. In ancient China, during the Qin Dynasty, Qin Shi Huang sent the then-famous alchemist and explorer Xu Fu in search of the elixir of longevity. He was accompanied by five hundred young men and an equal number of young women. They sailed the eastern seas, but unfortunately, never returned[54]. In ancient times, it was also believed that inhaling noble substances such as cinnabar, hematite, jade, or gold could make life longer. However, as we know, they do not actually do such a thing, and are often toxic.

Centuries have passed, and we now get to live in an era of wonderful rejuvenating creams and supplements (which, in large, don't actually bring the desired results). In 2018, Forbes claimed that the value of the American market of preparations, or 'anti-aging' market, has risen to $250 billion[53]. In America and worldwide, prominent upward trends can be observed in this field. We all want to live longer and look younger, sometimes at any cost.

Meanwhile, it turns out that the recipe for the elixir of youth can be found somewhere else, and it doesn't have to be expensive or risky. On the contrary, it can be healthy and completely free! It involves the activation of sirtuins during IF.

So, what are sirtuins? And what should we do to activate them?

Sirtuins are proteins found in most living organisms, including humans. They were first discovered in the 1970s by a scientist and geneticist named Amara Klara.

However, the understanding of sirtuins was then limited to the reproductive function of yeast. The first sirtuin was named SIR2. Somewhat later, in the early 1990s, scientists discovered the existence of structures similar to SIR2.

It came to light that each living organism has a different number of sirtuins. For example, bacteria have one sirtuin, yeasts have five, and mice and humans have seven.

Sirtuins play a vital role in many critical biological processes. They regulate metabolism, gene transcription, repair, and maintenance of our DNA. They also reduce inflammation in the body, reduce oxidative stress, slow down the aging process of our skin, and much more. Sirtuins are often called longevity genes, so if we use them skillfully, we will be able to delay the aging process significantly.

Sirtuins can only function in the presence of NAD+ (nicotinamide adenine dinucleotide). NAD+ is a coenzyme found in living cells. This coenzyme is essential for cell metabolism and many other biological processes.

If we compared our body to a large company or business, sirtuins would be the boss, and NAD+ the payroll department. One cannot function without the other. However, NAD+ levels decline with age, which also results in a reduction in sirtuin levels. Less money to pay the boss, less efficiency; or in other words, fewer NAD+, fewer sirtuins.

Most importantly, it was found that using IF and/or a 10-30% reduction in calories in the diet causes an increase in NAD+ in the cells of our bodies.

Scientific research conducted on mice - which, after all, have the same number of sirtuins as humans - showed that IF or calorie restriction prolongs life expectancy by up to 30%[55] [56]!

A vital factor in this process is increasing NAD+, which you can do through:

- IF
- calorie restriction
- exercise (all sorts, but especially jogging and interval exercises)
- a ketogenic diet - a high-fat diet that makes the body lose energy by burning fat (a low-carbohydrate diet will also have a similar effect)
- resveratrol [57]– a polyphenol, which has an antioxidant effect, protects us against many diseases, and extends our lifespan. We can find resveratrol in over seventy different plants and foods. These include: grapes, dark red wine, mulberry, black currants, peanut butter, peanuts, raisins, cocoa, and dark chocolate
- nicotinamide riboside (NR) - a dietary supplement, available in small amounts in food. NR is actually vitamin B3.

To sum up, you do not have to risk your health or life to slow down the aging process. It is enough for you to make small changes to contribute towards the 'elixir of longevity'.

Finally, I would like to quote a little joke that I heard while listening to a lecture from founding director of the 'Institute of Aging Research', Dr. Nir Barzilai[58]:

A centenarian comes to an insurance agent and asks:

CENTENARIAN: Could I take out a life insurance policy?

AGENT: (looking at him in disbelief) Unfortunately, it might be difficult... I don't know if we have policies for centenarians...

CENTENARIAN: How is that? After all, you insured my father last week...

AGENT: How old is your father?

CENTENARIAN: 120.

AGENT: In that case, come on Tuesday. I will prepare the documents for you to sign.

CENTENARIAN: Unfortunately, I'm busy on Tuesday.

AGENT: (looking at him in disbelief) How is that? What do you have to do?

CENTENARIAN: I'm going to my grandfather's wedding.

AGENT: How old is your grandfather?

CENTENARIAN: My grandfather is 150 years old.

AGENT: How is that possible?! He is 150 years old, and he still wants to marry?!

CENTENARIAN: But he didn't want to get married! It's just that... His parents put a lot of pressure on him...

young

Asia's story

My name is Asia, and I am 40 years old. I am happily married, and a mother to a 15-year-old girl named Dominika. I have made the most important decision in my life: deciding to fight my weaknesses.

My struggle was to change my diet to a healthier one and finally take care of how I look. The latter may not be the most important thing, but let's face it - our appearance can say a lot about us. My adventure with weight loss began on April 28, 2018, and continues until today.

It was an impulse decision - my weight had reached 93 kg with a height of 165 cm. Shocking! I felt sadness, anger, shame – because, I asked myself, how can you get yourself to that point? How? And...what next? What tools should I use to make it effective? Everyone can lose weight. But the hard part is: you have to maintain your weight.

I decided to begin my journey by trying Ewa Dąbrowska's 42-day fasting programme with vegetables and fruit. It was not easy. On the contrary, making the decision required a lot of willpower and persistence.

I knew that it would be a challenging stage of my life. After all, I had decided to fight, while not entirely believing in myself. After all, each time I had tried to lose weight, the kilograms returned - so I was not confident at all.

Before even beginning, I was wondering how this journey would end and whether I would achieve my goal. Will there be any setbacks along the way, and will I be able to get past them? I have always had the strong support of my husband (the person who motivated me the most, and at the same time, demotivated me because I had never heard a bad word about my appearance from his mouth. On the contrary, I would only hear superlatives!).

Well, the kilograms did start to disappear quickly. The effects were visible, my mood was fantastic, and the 42 days of fasting were over. There was still 'tough days', but it worked.

I have always read a lot and relied on the books written by Dąbrowska, MD. So, my next step was to finish the 42-day fasting period and find a way to lose even more kilograms, maintain the effect of the fast, and maintain healthy eating habits. I started keto-adaptation and living with ketosis. At the same time, I wanted to start ketogenic nutrition - which has since become my lifestyle.

Everything seemed clear to me up to then, until two magic letters appeared in front of my eyes: "IF". I thought that things might get complicated using IF, but I was wrong.

In the beginning, I was very skeptical about the idea of not eating for 16 hours (my eating window was 16/8, i.e., I ate from 11:00 am to 7:00 pm). I honestly admit that I even wondered who in their right mind would willingly like to go through such a hell. But that's all in the past now.

And now? Now I have achieved my goal - I lost the extra 40 kg, and most importantly, I keep maintaining my dream weight thanks to IF. My negative attitude towards this diet has changed. I eat for 8 hours (the required number of calories with 3 meals a day). However, I don't just eat whatever I want because that wouldn't work! During the next 16 hours, I do not eat at all. I only drink water, green tea, coffee, and it is absolutely doable - trust me.

I have control over my food. Food stopped controlling me. IF is a brilliant tool that has made me quit snacking between meals and caused a real revolution in my body. My stomach does not work all the time. I have a lot of energy, and I am "free" in the literal sense of the word. I do not have to snack and think about food constantly, and most importantly, I do not feel hungry for 16 hours. In the past, I have dealt with the relentless and unrestrained craving. Believe me, I am not pretending that I don't get hungry!

IF gives me pleasure and satisfaction. It has helped me avoid sweets, had a very positive effect on reducing my body fat, and as previously mentioned, freed me from obsessive thinking about eating for the rest of the day.

It also taught me to listen to my body's needs, and how to recognise real hunger and thirst. My body used to be hungry and thirsty all the time, now it is not the case.

To sum up my story, I feel I ruined my body (93 kg is quite a feat), and I am very ashamed of it. I sometimes cannot wrap my head around my old looks.

Thanks to the diet created by Dąbrowska, the ketogenic style of eating, physical activity, and IF, I have achieved everything I have

dreamed of. I have gained self-confidence, and I finally like myself the way I am - although I realise that self-control is the key to maintaining the results. I also know that it will never be easy.

The time has come for me to reveal a great secret to you: "repetition" is the key to achieving what I have achieved. I will definitely repeat the fasting suggested by Dąbrowska to cleanse my body. I also know that IF will be a part of my life forever, despite slight deviations from the norm (holidays, dinners with friends, birthday parties, or meetings with friends).

Everything is possible - I honestly believe this. it is enough to want something very much as long as you never give up. Do not talk about your plans out loud, but show your results instead. Success is often achieved silently when no one is watching.

I hope that my story will be helpful to you. Everything we do, we should do for ourselves. Never forget the phrase: "STRENGTH IS A WOMAN." I keep my fingers crossed for you, and whatever decision you make, I know it will be good. Stick to what you decide, and IF will help you on the way.

It will be your invisible friend, and the hands of the clock will be your lodestar. Dreams do not come true by themselves; we need to make them happen. It does not matter whether our dreams have to do with our passion, love, work, people or things. It all comes down to work and actions. It is impossible to move forward if we do not have the courage to take the first step. You cannot maintain something if you do not take care of it. I have made it - now it is your turn!

Łukasz's story

Hi, I would like to tell you about my little metamorphosis.

Age-35, height-190cm, weight in March 2018 - 86 kg

Now-81 kg

I have been using IF for over a year and I sincerely recommend it.

My eating window is 7/17, and 8/16 at weekends.

I eat everything. I try to keep low levels of carbs and high levels of protein. And I do not eat sweets because I do not like them. However, I drink beer and wine at weekends - the effects would be much better if I didn't.

I am on a slight caloric deficit: I eat 2600kcl, and my required number of calories is 2900kcl, so it is -300kcl. I want to recompose my body and, at the moment, go down to 9-11% of body fat.

I do interval training 3-4 times a week for about 40-50, minutes as well as push-ups, squats, chin-ups, planks, etc. I also run very short distances without any breaks. There is still a lot of work ahead of me, but I should achieve my goals next year.

(I will also add that my gynecomastia is disappearing on one side, and my GP was once sure that it required a surgical procedure!)

I have already tested almost everything diet wise; the results were poor and hard to maintain. My frame of mind is much better now that I have switched to Intermittent Fasting. I am 1,000,000% sure that everyone can do it, because I have been very successful. Just stick to your calories, IF, and exercise. You do not need the gym or any special equipment. Your body weight is enough. This system really works wonders.

Regards.

Eat what you want and look the way you want - it is not a scam!

Ewa's story

My adventure with IF began on October 1, 2018. My previous attempts to fight my obesity failed or had a very short-term effect (or 'yo-yo' effect).

A YouTube video that I accidentally found helped me a lot. In the video, the author just mentioned the Intermittent Fasting eating style.

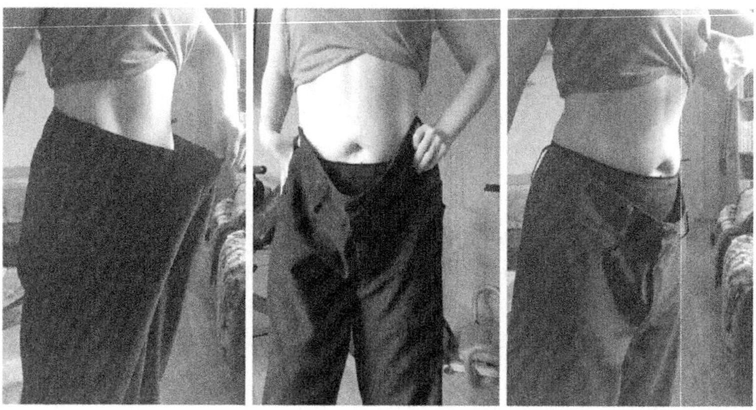

After finding out more about IF, I decided to implement the system into my life. I determined my daily required number of calories and cut down on calories to make a deficit. I also limited anything unhealthy in my diet to the occasional minimum and introduced 3 training sessions a week.

After a few days of adapting to the new lifestyle (yes, I can say now that it is my lifestyle), my body adjusted.

After a month, I began to feel and notice the first effects of the changes that I had introduced.

First of all, I learned not to worry about scales (this device is a source of unnecessary pressure for me). The indicator of success has been my clothes and centimeters in my circumferences - my clothing size used to be 44/46 (European sizing), and now it is 34/36.

Secondly, thanks to IF, I became aware of what I had eaten before and in what quantity. I realised that we eat huge amounts of empty calories every day. Also, we do it not because we are hungry, but because... we can.

Thirdly, I have never felt such freedom while being on any other diet. Knowing that the two meals I eat a day can be enough turned eating into a pleasure. Before that, my meals used to be low in calories. They were also a real ordeal for me.

I eat what I want, but I always keep in mind the required number of calories. IF has been an invaluable help for me during my journey to find a better version of myself.

Arek C.'s story

IF: if you want, you can do it!

IF gives you an obscure option to keep your body fat under control.

This is what prompted me to try this eating system.

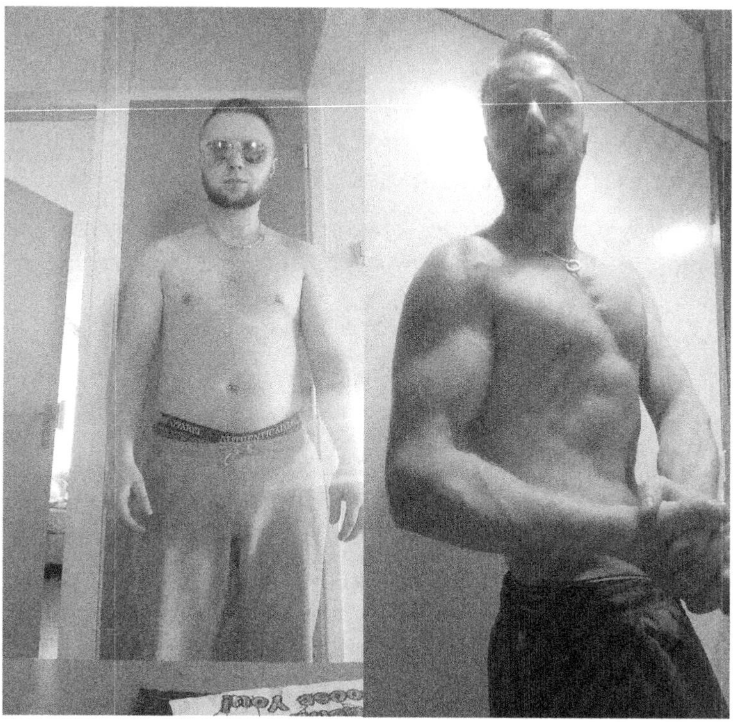

I am an amateur who weight trains. It is my little world and although I do not intend to compete anywhere, or in any competitions, I have my 'silhouette' goals.

I am 36 and have been using IF for 3 years with longer and shorter eating windows.

I extended my fasting periods before the summer holidays, around January 2019, for up to 20 hours a day. The adaptation of the body is pretty simple if you are not new to IF, you know your body and its needs. You also need to be able to eat intuitively.

Currently, I do not even count my calories. For over a few good months, I have been testing different calories and macros on myself. It is essential to keep your protein high, whether you are doing mass or reduction.

IF will be with me permanently because it gives me a lot of freedom when it comes to my daily schedule. You do not have to spend time cooking in the morning or devour your breakfast quickly.

You will be able to see that I eat everything and do myself proud on my Instagram account (@cheatmealfitbody). IF burns excess fat during fasting, and I enjoy eating with no restrictions. IF gives you freedom and creates good eating habits that most people lack these days.

Best regards, Arek C.

Monika's story

My experience with IF:

My name is Monika. I am 39 years old and have two children. I have always had weight problems. I have tried many diets with varying results.

In February 2019, I started to get interested in IF. Honestly, I was obese, and I felt terrible about my body. I would come home from work, cook dinner, eat it with my family, and then go to bed. I sometimes fell asleep while sitting and watching TV, and I lacked energy.

I was trying to find a miracle cure on the internet back then, and I found IF. It really drew me in, and I read all the available information on the topic. I was very desperate - I took pictures of myself just to see how others saw me; it scared me.

I remember that I climbed on the scales one evening and saw 79.5 kg - it was horrible. I started using IF almost every day - first the 16/8 variant.

A healthy diet mattered. I prepared everything myself, and I did not count calories. In fact, I ate everything that I wanted. I limited sweets and ready-made food. I carefully followed my fasting periods. The kilograms started to drop, and I felt really great; I had more energy.

I adjusted fasting to my lifestyle. I start work at 6 a.m., so I started fasting at 4 p.m. and finished at 8 a.m. When my body was ready, I increased the number of hours during which I fasted. At the moment, I use the 20/4 method 7 days a week.

I noticed that giving up sweetened coffee and tea, milk, or sweeteners is really important during fasting. I also started to move more: gym classes 3-4 times a week.

At the moment I have lost 18 kg. Though I still have to work on myself, I feel much better, finally feminine, and I like myself now. IF is a lifestyle that is with me every day.

Whenever I have bad days, reading and seeing other people's photos and results motivate me - I do it almost every night. That's why at some point I decided to show my transformation - it may help someone else.

Arek K.'s story

I started my adventure with IF by accident, while using another slimming diet.

During the summer, I decided that I weighed too much and that it was time to lose some weight. It started quite typically, as for many people - with a low-calorie diet combined with exercise. I also put aside beer because after drinking it, I would get a ravenous appetite. I ate five meals a day, spread throughout the day, of course.

The diet was effective, and I lost a few kilograms. However, I realised that it was not for me, mainly due to the lack of time to prepare so many meals and because I worked shifts.

I struggled the most while working the night shifts all week long. So, I started searching the Internet for news about different diets, and I accidentally watched a video on IF.

At first, I was pretty skeptical about it, probably because the rules of this diet contradicted the knowledge that I had for years. However, the concept of IF interested me, and I kept investigating. The rules, on the other hand, seemed simple. Eat for 8 hours and fast for 16.

I decided to try it. Somehow, I did it without any major problems. I arranged the eating windows according to my work shifts. The weight started to drop, and I felt good.

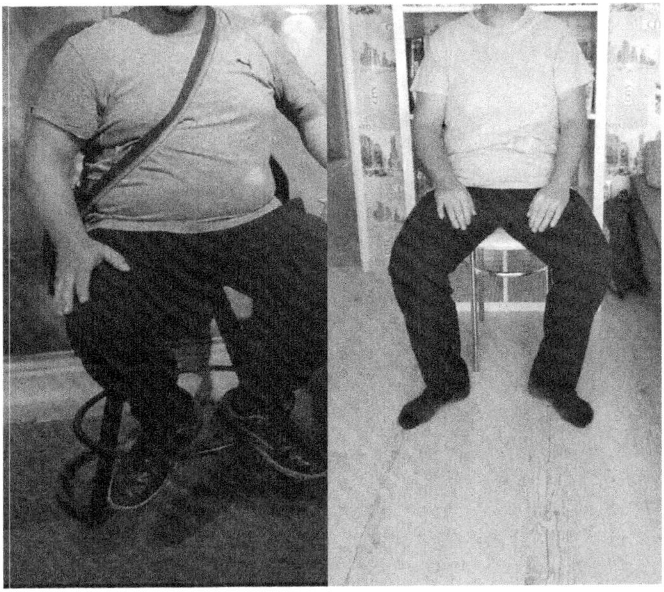

My digestive system responded in a very positive way. Of course, there were also some deviations, such as some sweets or alcohol. However, after a setback, I would return to IF again. So far, I have managed to lose 15 kg, which makes me very happy. I am planning to lose more, and most importantly, maintain my weight.

What does IF give me? First of all, I do not have to think about food or prepare a few small meals. I do not have to deny myself anything, which was true for other diets. I eat what I like, but I avoid junk food. An important aspect is the fact that you do not have to "abandon" IF - you can simply stick to it and use it all the time. I recommend it to people who have problems with losing weight.

Wioletta's story

My name is Wioletta. I am 27 years old, 158 cm tall, and my weight is 58 kg. I am a mother of a boy who is a year and a half old - I had a caesarean section to give birth. I suffer from neurosis, compulsive eating disorder, postpartum depression, and hypothyroidism.

My story begins in early childhood. I am not going to blame it on my genes, but the truth is, the tendency to put on weight is hereditary in my case. However, this is not true for my mother who can eat whatever she wants and does not get fat.

Since childhood, a person close to me has been telling me that I was too fat. However, looking at old photos, I can objectively say that I was of an average body build. Additionally, I was "friends" with a toxic person. Fortunately, after several years, I was able to free myself from that person.

I have tried all possible diets, slimming teas, slimming belts, corsets, creams, and other wonderful methods. They either did not work, or the effects were temporary. Whenever I managed to keep my diet and be more active, one stressful situation at home or work was enough to make me go back to gluttony and eating my feelings.

It helped, but for a moment, and then remorse did not let me live. I felt ugly and worthless. I became obsessed with counting calories, and then I actually lost weight, but at a high cost - anemia, extreme body weakness, migraines, vomiting.

Then came years of ups and downs. I was pregnant and 75 kg with a height of 158 cm. Depression - immediately after the caesarean I lost 13 kg. After taking antidepressants, I felt better mentally, and my appetite returned.

When my weight was 67.8 kg, I accidentally came across some information, promoting what some said was "utter nonsense". That information contradicted everything that nutritionists and doctors had been telling me for years. I decided to take a chance, one last time.

I started by reducing the number of meals first, giving up dairy, and then cutting down on carbohydrates. Finally, I felt ready to give IF a shot. And it was a great choice.

I was active, ate fewer meals and carbs, and fasted. My weight and centimeters started to disappear super-fast, my complexion improved. Thanks to interval exercises and pilates, my body became firmer, and my buttocks were lifted.

I get ill less frequently, sleep better, and have more energy. I finally understand the difference between physical and mental hunger. My only concern is my stomach. I try to fast during the week, and at weekends I eat a bit less rigorously.

I still feel down from time to time and eat more, but I do it less often. And finally, I do not spend my whole day in the kitchen because I eat 1-2 (sometimes 3) meals a day.

This is the first "diet" that I want to stick to forever because it is effective, practical, and straightforward. I used to wear the UK size 14/12, but now I wear 10.

IF has definitely increased my self-esteem to a large extent. For the first time in years, I wore a one-piece swimsuit at the swimming pool.

I know that I will achieve my goal if I am consistent.

I can safely say that IF changed my life and saved me.

I am a happy mother and wife now.

Frequently Asked Questions.

Is it necessary to cut calories during an eating window to lose weight?

Intermittent Fasting 16:8 has a massive advantage, because your body begins to draw energy from stored fat after 13-15 hours. Therefore, it speeds up the weight loss process. However, a low caloric deficit is recommended to make the weight loss process as effective as possible. Also, if you intend to lose weight, you need a caloric deficit. If you just want to keep your weight, you do not need the deficit. Yet, a slight weight loss may occur in the latter case as well.

I have been using the toilet more often since I started using IF, why is that?

This is quite normal, especially when starting using IF. There are three reasons why this happens. First, when your body begins taking energy from fat, it also produces ketone bodies that increase diuresis. Secondly, your body's reserves of glycogen are depleted, releasing water from your body. Thirdly, an average person starting their journey with IF increases the amount of water they drink to cope with hunger, which in turn increases excretion.

What is OMAD?

OMAD stands for 'one meal a day.' A person using the OMAD method gets all the required calories within a 1-hour eating window.

Can I have eating windows/fast alongside training sessions?

It all depends on what type of training or exercise you are considering. When it comes to cardio, the further along you are during the IF process, the better. A particular research study in Germany found that the longer you do not eat, the more effective it will be to burn fat, especially around the belly area.

When it comes to weight training, fasting will also bring you tremendous benefits. You can learn more about this in the Growth Hormone section. A world-renowned celebrity trainer and IF specialist Thomas DeLauer recommends that you do weight exercises during fasting and keep fasting afterwards. DeLauer follows this principle himself, and as you can see, this approach brings him great results. Yet, opinions on this matter differ in the world of sport.

Can you add coconut oil to your coffee during fasting?

No, you cannot. The acceptable drinks are listed in this book.

What can you eat during your eating window?

During your eating window, you can rely on your favourite diet, such as ketogenic, vegetarian, carnivorous, paleo or low-carb diet. You can choose whatever diet you prefer. However, you should think your diet through because you need to be sure that you provide all the necessary nutrients for the proper functioning of your body, considering a reduced number of meals.

Does sugar-free chewing gum disrupt fasting?

This topic is explored in the book.

Does IF make our metabolism slow down?

IF does not slow down metabolism, quite the contrary. When do you feel you have more energy? Are you more energetic during IF or maybe after six meals a day and continuous snacking? Your body will be more motivated during fasting. Let's think of our Palaeolithic ancestors who did not have fridges. Their senses must have been very acute to allow them to find food. Also, metabolism does not decrease during IF.

Additionally, research conducted on fasting confirms this claim. An example of such a research study was published in January 2019 by Okinawa University. The scientists found that IF generates increased metabolic activity in the body.

Is it possible to lose weight using IF without exercise?

Yes, it is. It is essential to realise that 70% of success in losing weight comes down to a properly selected diet and 30% to physical activity. It should also be noted here that physical activity does not entail just exercise. Physical activity can mean a walk, doing house chores (you can get tired while doing them!), playing with children, and so on...

Is it true that I can get bad breath during IF?

In sporadic cases, an unpleasant odour from the mouth may occur. This is due to the increased number of ketone bodies in the body.

If you experience such an adverse effect, try to drink more water. You can also chew on clove to neutralise the bad smell from the mouth.

Do I always have to eat at the same time, and what if I'm working shifts?

Professor Satchin Panda explains that it is better to eat at the same time, so as not to change the biological cycle of our organs constantly. Research on this subject conducted by three American scientists was awarded the prestigious Nobel Prize in 2017.

Keeping identical eating windows is not an easy task these days, especially for shift workers. While working shifts, for example night work, eat only a light meal during the night. After returning home in the morning, have a small breakfast before going to bed. Remember to get enough sleep, because a lack of it may contribute to problems with achieving your weight goals.

I had a coffee with my friends, and although I was not going to eat anything, I was tempted by the cheesecake during my fasting hours. What should I do? Help!

IF is for everyone. We must adjust it so that it does not turn us into social recluses. Unless you eat the cheesecake regularly, such outings are acceptable. Go back to your normal IF routine the next day.

How long can I use Intermittent Fasting?

IF, unlike dieting, is a lifelong eating style. Of course, IF is not recommended in certain cases, like pregnancy, for example. This book contains a complete list of instances where abandoning this style of life is advisable.

Can I combine the 16:8 variant with the 5:2 method?

Yes, you can combine the two systems. For two days when you use the 5:2 variant, you eat 500-800 calories. On the other hand, during the days with the 16:8 method, you should not have a caloric deficit.

What is a cheat day?

It is a day when you go a little crazy despite being on a diet. Once a week or biweekly, you do not need to maintain your caloric deficit. You can even have a slight caloric surplus. However, you must be careful not to go too crazy, because you certainly do not want to ruin the efforts of the whole week.

I am going to a wedding reception, what should I do?

Do it and have a great time. Treat the wedding reception as your "cheat day". Go back to your standard eating window the following day.

Do I need to be on a keto diet while using IF?

No, IF does not dictate what diet you should follow. You can be on any diet of your choice.

Is there any proven app for counting calories and macronutrients?

Yes. Two trendy calorie counting applications are MyFitnessPal and Fitatu.

Do I have to count macros during IF?

No, you do not. However, many people care about macros because of their muscle gain goals or specific dietary goals.

Is there an app to summarise my daily macronutrients?

Yes, Fitatu is one of them.

References

1. Yoshinori Ohsumi, Y. (2016). *The Nobel Prize in Physiology or Medicine 2016*, https://www.nobelprize.org/prizes/medicine/2016/press-release/ Accessed August 21, 2019

2. Takeshige, K., Baba, M., Tsuboi, S., Noda, T. and Ohsumi, Y. (1992). *Autophagy in yeast demonstrated with proteinase-deficient mutants and conditions for its induction.* Journal of Cell Biology 119, 301-311.

3. Mizushima, N., Noda, T., Yoshimori, T., Tanaka, Y., Ishii, T., George, M.D., Klionsky, D.J., Ohsumi, M. and Ohsumi, Y. (1998). *A protein conjugation system essential for autophagy.* Nature 395, 395-398.

4. Tinsley GM, La Bounty PM, Y. (2015). *Effects of intermittent fasting on body composition and clinical health markers in humans.* 73, 661-74.

5. Varady KA, Bhutani S, Church EC, Klempel MC, Y. (2009). *Short-term modified alternate-day fasting: a novel dietary strategy for weight loss and cardioprotection in obese adults.* Oxford University in The American Journal of Clinical Nutrition, Vol 90, Issue 5, November 2009, Pages 1138–1143

6. Hiroshi Sogawa, Chiharu Kubo, Y. (2000). *Influence of short-term repeated fasting on the longevity of female (NZB×NZW)F1 mice,* Mechanisms of Ageing and Development, Vol. 115, Issues 1–2, 61-71.

7. Naomi Whittel, William Dunn, Y. (2019) *Autophagy 101 – Everything You Need to Know – with Dr. William Dunn,* https://www.youtube.com/watch?v=ERKmJK_atdc Accessed August 21, 2019

8. Mindy Peltz, Y. (2019). *4 Strategies to Get Into Autophagy,* https://www.youtube.com/watch?v=dhUR9cWTpbo Accessed August 21, 2019

9. Shuhei Nakamura, Tamotsu Yoshimori, Y. (2018). *Autophagy and Longetivity,* Molecules and Cells, 65-72

10. Y. (2003). *The Chemistry of Amino Acids,* The Biology Project, Department of Biochemistry and Molecular Biophysics, University of Arizona.

11. Tinsley GM, La Bounty PM, Y. (2015). *Effects of intermittent fasting on body composition and clinical health markers in humans,* Oxford university in Nutrition Reviews Vol 73, Issue 10, pages 661-674

12. Terra G Arnason, Matthew W Bowen, Kerry D Mansell, Y. (2017) *Effects of intermittent fasting on health markers in those with type 2 diabetes: A pilot study,* World J Diabetes, 154-164

13. Peter R. Kerndt, MD, James L. Naughton, MD, Charles E. Driscoll, MD, and David A. Loxterkamp, MD, Y. (1982). *Fasting: The History, Pathophysiology and Complications,* West J Med, 379–399

14. M L Hartman, J D Veldhuis, M L Johnson, M M Lee, K G Alberti, E Samojlik, M O Thorner, Y. (1992). *Augmented growth hormone (GH) secretory burst frequency and amplitude mediate enhanced GH secretion during a two-day fast in normal men,* The Journal of Clinical Endocrinology & Metabolism, Vol 74, Issue 4, Pages 757–765

15. Kian Y Ho, Johannes D. Veldhuls, Michael L. Johnson, Richard Furlanetto, William S. Evans, K. G. M. M. Alberti, Michael O. Thorner, Y. (1988). *Fasting Enhances Growth Hormone Secretion and Amplifies the Complex Rhythms of Growth Hormone Secretion in Man.* The American Society for Clinical Investigation, Inc., Vol 81, 968-975

16. Stephanie R. Edmondson, Susan P. Thumiger, George A. Werther, Christopher J. Eright, Y. (2003), *Epidermal Homeostasis: The Role of the Growth Hormone and Insulin-Like Growth Factor Systems,* Endocrine Reviews, Vol 24, Issue 6, 737-764

17. Moline ML, Monk TH, Wagner DR, Pollak CP, Kream J, Fookson JE, Weitzman ED, Czeisler CA, Y. (1986), *Human growth hormone release is decreased during sleep in temporal isolation (free-running),* Vol 1, Issue 13, 13-9

18. Mateusz Klimczak, Y. (2019) *"Cukier, otyłość – konsekwencje" – prezentacja raportu,* Ministerstwo Zdrowia, https://www.gov.pl/web/zdrowie/cukier-otylosc-konsekwencje-prezentacja-raportu Accessed August 21, 2019

19. Michael Mosley, Mimi Spencer, Y. (2015), *The Fast Diet*, Simon and Schuster

20. Jason Fung, Andreas Eenfeldt, Y. (2015), *The Perfect Treatment for Type 2 Diabetes*, https://www.youtube.com/watch?v=oFJ5Sv5ifes Accessed August 21, 2019

21. Jillian Levy, CHHC, Y. (2018), *Benefits & Dangers of IGF-1: Weight-Loss Promoter or Cancer Causer?*, Dr. Axe, https://draxe.com/health/endocrine-system/igf-1/ Accessed August 21, 2019

22. Key TJ, Y. (2011), *Diet, insulin-like growth factor-1 and cancer risk*, Proceedings of the Nutrition Society, Issue May 3, 1-4

23. Y. (2019), *Paleolityczny styl życia*, Wikipedia, https://pl.wikipedia.org/wiki/Paleolityczny_styl_życia Accessed August 21, 2019

24. Damian Wiatrowski, Y. (2016), *Hormonalna kontrola wagi - śniadanie białkowo tłuszczowe*, https://www.youtube.com/watch?v=j7HqRR66Zfg Accessed August 21, 2019

25. Mindy Peltz, Y. (2017), *Hunger - How to Turn off your Hunger Hormones*, https://www.youtube.com/watch?v=5skC8zfXEK8 Accessed August 21, 2019

26. Philip Hunter, Y. (2012), *The inflammation theory of*

disease, EMBO Reports, Vol 13, Issue 11, 968-970

27. Harper AE, Miller RH, Block KP, Y. (1984), *Branched-chain amino acid metabolism*, Annual Review of Nutrition, Vol 4, 409-54

28. Alpana P. Shukla, Radu G. Iliescu, Catherine E. Thomas, Louis J. Aronne, Y. (2015), *Food Order Has a Significant Impact on Postprandial Glucose and Insulin Levels*, Diabetes Care, Issue 38

29. Weigle DS, Breen PA, Matthys CC, Callahan HS, Meeuws KE, Burden VR, Purnell JQ, Y. (2005), *A high-protein diet induces sustained reductions in appetite, ad libitum caloric intake, and body weight despite compensatory changes in diurnal plasma leptin and ghrelin concentrations.*, The American Journal of Clinical Nutrition, Vol 82, 41-8

30. Leidy HJ, Tang M, Armstrong CL, Martin CB, Campbell WW, Y. (2011), *The effects of consuming frequent, higher protein meals on appetite and satiety during weight loss in overweight/obese men*, Obesity (Silver Spring), Vol 19, 818-24

31. Li L, Li X, Zhou W, Messina JL, Y. (2013), *Acute psychological stress results in the rapid development of insulin resistance.*, The Journal of Endocrinology, 175-84

32. Yu-Xiang Yan, Huan-Bo Xiao, Si-Si Wang, Jing Zhao, Yan He, Wei Wang, Jing Dong, Y. (2016), *Investigation of the Relationship Between Chronic Stress and Insulin Resistance*

in a Chinese Population, The Journal of Epidemiology, Vol 26, Issue 7, 355-360

33. Just T, Pau HW, Engel U, Hummel T, Y. (2008), *Cephalic phase insulin release in healthy humans after taste stimulation?,* Appetite, Vol 51, Issue 3, 622-627

34. Tonosaki K, Hori Y, Shimizu Y, Tonosaki K, Y. (2007), *Relationships between insulin release and taste.,* Biomedical Research, Tokyo, Japan Vol 28, Issue 2, 79-83

35. Medical Research Council. (2019), *How eating feeds into the body clock.* ScienceDaily. https://www.sciencedaily.com/releases/2019/04/190425143607.htm Accessed November 15, 2019

36. Panda.S, Y. (2018). *The Circadian Code: Lose weight, supercharge your energy and sleep well every night,* Vermillion

37. Garaulet M, Gómez-Abellán P, Alburquerque-Béjar JJ, Lee YC, Ordovás JM, Scheer FA, Y. (2013), *Timing of food intake predicts weight loss effectiveness.,* International Journal of Obesity 37, 604-611

38. Marcheva B, Ramsey KM, Buhr ED, Kobayashi Y, Su H, Ko CH, Ivanova G, Omura C, Mo S, Vitaterna MH, Lopez JP, Philipson LH, Bradfield CA, Crosby SD, JeBailey L, Wang X, Takahashi JS, Bass J, Y. (2010), *Disruption of the clock components CLOCK and BMAL1 leads to hypoinsulinaemia and diabetes,* Nature 466, 627-631

39. Qian J, Block GD, Colwell CS, Matveyenko AV, Y. (2013), *Consequences of Exposure to Light at Night on the Pancreatic Islet Circadian Clock and Function in Rats,* Diabetes, 3469-78

40. Zembaty M, Porter J, Y. (1984) *Siedem życzeń,* BOX Music

41. Perkins D, Y. (2019), *Najbardziej Regularne i Najczęściej Stosowane Rodzaje Intermittent Fasting,* Facebook, https://www.facebook.com/groups/161198694495436/permalink/437707110177925/ Accessed November 16, 2019

42. Y. (2019) *Hipokrates,* PWN, https://encyklopedia.pwn.pl/haslo/Hipokrates;3911863.html Accessed November 16, 2019

43. Y. (2019), *Paracelsus,* Wikipedia, https://pl.wikipedia.org/wiki/Paracelsus Accessed November 16, 2019

44. Y. (2019), *Post,* Wikipedia, https://pl.wikipedia.org/wiki/Post Accessed November 16, 2019

45. Pawel J, Y. (1983), *Dni i Okresy Pokutne w Kosciele,* Kodeks Prawa Kanonicznego, kan 1249-1253

46. Post, Bibliamowi.pl, https://bibliamowi.pl/zagadnienie/post-2/ Accessed November 16, 2019

47. Mawlawi F, *Post w Ramadanie,* Muzulmanski Zwiazek Religijny w RP Najwyzsze Kolegium Muzulmanskie, http://mzr.pl/post/ Accessed November 16, 2019

48. Y. (2012), *Post przed świętem Zaśnięcia Bogurodzicy,* Parafia Prawosławna św. Jana Klimaka na woli w Warszawie, https://prawoslawie.pl/aktualnosci/36-post-uspienski Accessed November 16, 2019

49. Rzym M, Y. (2017), *Post w religiach świata,* Misyjne.pl, https://misyjne.pl/post-religiach-swiata/ Accessed November 16, 2019

50. Berg E, Y. (2017), *Can You Drink Coffee With Intermittent Fasting? And Other Acceptable Liquids*, YouTube, https://youtu.be/6aOGxhbe-Hc Accessed November 16, 2019

51. Eenfeldt A, Fung J, Y. (2019), *Intermittent fasting – questions & answers,* Diet Doctor, https://www.dietdoctor.com/intermittent-fasting/questions-and-answers Accessed November 16, 2019

52. DeLauer T, Y. (2018), *How to Do a Bone Broth Fast: Benefits and Schedule,* YouTube, https://www.youtube.com/watch?v=qfMAwm2oHcA Accessed November 16, 2019

53. Barsouk A, Y. (2018), *The Cure to Aging Could Be Hiding in Plain Sight,* Forbes,

https://www.forbes.com/sites/adambarsouk/2018/10/21/the-cure-to-aging-could-be-hiding-in-plain-sight/#3c52f70a7041 Accessed January 12, 2020

54. Y. (2019), *Elixir of Life*, Wikipedia, https://en.wikipedia.org/wiki/Elixir_of_life Accessed January 12, 2020

55. Salehi B, Mishra AP, Nigam M, et al., Y. (2018) *Resveratrol: A Double-Edged Sword in Health Benefits.*, Biomedicines. Vol 6(3), 91

56. Barzilai N, Y. (2013) *Is There A Longevity Gene? The Biology of Aging with Nir Barzilai, MD*, YouTube, https://www.youtube.com/watch?v=wKcqVJVdi84 Accessed January 14 2020

57. Guarente L, Y. (2012) *Anti-Aging Genes*, YouTube, https://www.youtube.com/watch?v=L29J6_Brn-A Accessed January 14 2020

58. Giblin W, Skinner ME, Lombard DB., Y. (2014) *Sirtuins: guardians of mammalian healthspan.*, Trends in Genetics. Vol 30(7), 271–286.

59. Hipokrates, Paracelsus https://www.azquotes.com/author/22138-Hippocrates https://www.azquotes.com/author/11295-Paracelsus Accessed November 16, 2019

60. Post w judaizmie, Wikipedia,

https://pl.wikipedia.org/wiki/Post#Post_w_judaizmie
Accessed November 12, 2019

61. Stephan P. Bauersfeld, Christian S. Kessler, Manfred Wischnewsky, Annette Jaensch, Nico Steckhan, Rainer Stange, Barbara Kunz, Barbara Brückner, Jalid Sehouli and Andreas Michalsen, Y.(2018),
The effects of short-term fasting on quality of life and tolerance to chemotherapy in patients with breast and ovarian cancer: a randomized cross-over pilot study,
https://valterlongo.com/wp-content/uploads/2018/11/2018_Breast-and-Ovarian-Cancer_BMC-Cancer_Bauersfeld.pdf

Thank you for buying my book!

It would mean a lot to me to hear from you and get your review on Amazon.

You can scan this QR code to take you to your review page on Amazon.

If you wish to join my Polish Intermittent Fasting group, scan here:

Best Wishes
Dorota Perkins
2021

Printed in Great Britain
by Amazon

23883978R00090